THE HOME FRONT: GERMANY

This volume is one of a series that chronicles
in full the events of the Second World War.
Previous books in the series include:

Prelude to War
Blitzkrieg
The Battle of Britain
The Rising Sun
The Battle of the Atlantic
Russia Besieged
The War in the Desert
The Home Front: U.S.A.
China-Burma-India
Island Fighting
The Italian Campaign
Partisans and Guerrillas
The Second Front
Liberation
Return to the Philippines
The Air War in Europe
The Resistance
The Battle of the Bulge
The Road to Tokyo
Red Army Resurgent
The Nazis
Across the Rhine
War under the Pacific
War in the Outposts
The Soviet Juggernaut
Japan at War
The Mediterranean
Battles for Scandinavia
The Secret War
Prisoners of War
The Commandos

WORLD WAR II · TIME-LIFE BOOKS · ALEXANDRIA, VIRGINIA

BY CHARLES WHITING
AND THE EDITORS OF TIME-LIFE BOOKS

THE HOME FRONT: GERMANY

Time-Life Books Inc.
is a wholly owned subsidiary of
TIME INCORPORATED

Founder: Henry R. Luce 1898-1967

Editor-in-Chief: Henry Anatole Grunwald
President: J. Richard Munro
Chairman of the Board: Ralph P. Davidson
Executive Vice President: Clifford J. Grum
Chairman, Executive Committee: James R. Shepley
Editorial Director: Ralph Graves
Group Vice President, Books: Joan D. Manley
Vice Chairman: Arthur Temple

TIME-LIFE BOOKS INC.

Managing Editor: Jerry Korn
Text Director: George Constable
Board of Editors: Dale M. Brown, George G. Daniels,
Thomas H. Flaherty Jr., Martin Mann,
Philip W. Payne, Gerry Schremp, Gerald Simons, Kit
van Tulleken
Planning Director: Edward Brash
Art Director: Tom Suzuki
   Assistant: Arnold C. Holeywell
Director of Administration: David L. Harrison
Director of Operations: Gennaro C. Esposito
Director of Research: Carolyn L. Sackett
   Assistant: Phyllis K. Wise
Director of Photography: Dolores A. Littles

Chairman: John D. McSweeney
President: Carl G. Jaeger
Executive Vice Presidents: John Steven Maxwell,
David J. Walsh
Vice Presidents: George Artandi, Stephen L. Bair,
Peter G. Barnes, Nicholas Benton, John L. Canova,
Beatrice T. Dobie, Carol Flaumenhaft,
James L. Mercer, Herbert Sorkin, Paul R. Stewart

WORLD WAR II

Editor: Thomas H. Flaherty Jr.
Senior Editors: Anne Horan, Henry Woodhead
Designer: Herbert H. Quarmby
Chief Researcher: Philip Brandt George

Editorial Staff for *The Home Front: Germany*
Picture Editor: Jeremy Ross
Text Editors: Robert Menaker, Richard Murphy
Writers: Patricia C. Bangs, Donald Davison Cantlay,
Richard D. Kovar
Researchers: Mary G. Burns, Scarlet Cheng,
Reginald H. Dickerson, Jane S. Hanna,
Trudy W. Pearson, Marta Ann Sanchez,
Paula York-Soderlund
Copy Coordinators: Ann Bartunek, Allan Fallow,
Elizabeth Graham, Barbara F. Quarmby
Art Assistant: Mikio Togashi
Picture Coordinator: Betty Hughes Weatherley
Editorial Assistant: Andrea E. Reynolds

Special Contributors
Rosemary George, Susan Parsons (translations)

Editorial Operations
Production Director: Feliciano Madrid
   Assistants: Peter A. Inchauteguiz,
   Karen A. Meyerson
Copy Processing: Gordon E. Buck
Quality Control Director: Robert L. Young
   Assistant: James J. Cox
   Associates: Daniel J. McSweeney,
   Michael G. Wight
Art Coordinator: Anne B. Landry
Copy Room Director: Susan B. Galloway
   Assistants: Celia Beattie, Ricki Tarlow

Correspondents: Elisabeth Kraemer (Bonn); Margot
Hapgood, Dorothy Bacon (London); Susan Jonas,
Lucy T. Voulgaris (New York); Maria Vincenza Aloisi,
Josephine du Brusle (Paris); Ann Natanson (Rome).
Valuable assistance was also provided by: Wibo van
de Linde (Amsterdam); Helga Kohl, Angelika
Lemmer, Wanda Menke-Glückert (Bonn); Katrina
Van Duyn (Copenhagen); Robert Kroon (Geneva);
Marlin Levin (Jerusalem); Pippa Pridham (London);
Miriam Hsia, Christina Lieberman (New York);
M. T. Hirschkoff (Paris); Eva Stichova (Prague);
Bianca Gabbrielli (Rome); Traudl Lessing (Vienna).

The Author: CHARLES WHITING, a British writer specializing in World War II history, served during the war years with an armored reconnaissance regiment in Europe. Educated at two English universities, Leeds and London, as well as in Germany, Whiting was for six years the German correspondent of *The London Times Educational Supplement*. His books include *Patton, Battle of the Ruhr Pocket, Hunt for Martin Bormann, Death of a Division* and *Attack on Siegfried*.

The Consultants: COLONEL JOHN R. ELTING, USA (Ret.), a military historian, is the author of *The Battle of Bunker's Hill, The Battles of Saratoga, Military History and Atlas of the Napoleonic Wars* and, for the Time-Life Books World War II series, *Battles for Scandinavia*. The editor of *Military Uniforms in America: The Era of the American Revolution, 1755-1795* and *Military Uniforms in America: Years of Growth, 1796-1851*, he was also associate editor of *The West Point Atlas of American Wars*.

GEORGE O. KENT is a professor of European and German history at the University of Maryland. A former historian with the U.S. Air Force, the State Department and the Library of Congress, he is the author of *Arnim and Bismarck, Bismarck in His Time* and several articles on the Third Reich. He also edited a four-volume catalogue of German Foreign Ministry documents that were issued from 1920 to 1945.

Library of Congress Cataloguing in Publication Data

Whiting, Charles, 1926-
   The home front: Germany.

   (World War II; V. 32)
   Bibliography: p. 202
   Includes index.
   1. World War, 1939-1945—Germany. 2. Germany—
History—1933-1945.   I. Time-Life Books.
II. Title.   III. Series.
D757.H65   940.54'84'43   81-21406
ISBN 0-8094-3409-1
ISBN 0-8094-3408-3 (lib. bdg.)
ISBN 0-8094-3419-9 (retail ed.)

For information about any Time-Life book, please write:

Reader Information
Time-Life Books
541 North Fairbanks Court
Chicago, Illinois 60611

CONTENTS

HITLER'S CHILDREN

Grim beyond their years, boys belonging to the Hitler Youth turn eyes right at a Nazi rally. Their belt buckles carry the stern motto, "Blood and honor."

A GENERATION OF BELIEVERS

Leader Baldur von Schirach sits among his charges in 1938. "Every Hitler Youth," he exhorted, "carries a marshal's baton in his knapsack."

On May 1, 1945, with Hitler dead, Berlin fallen and the Third Reich in its final throes, some British troops advancing from the Baltic coast found themselves in an unexpected confrontation with a German defending the city of Wismar. "He was 11 years old and in short pants, and he wouldn't stop crying *'Heil Hitler!'* and shouting in broken English that Germany would still win the War," one of the soldiers recalled. "So in the end me and a couple of mates grabbed him by the legs, upturned him, stuck his head in a lavatory bowl, pulled the chain and flooded his face with water."

The forlorn child in that unsettling episode reflected the fierce loyalty that youthful Germans in particular gave to Adolf Hitler and the Reich he personified. For more than a decade the Führer had held a hammer lock on the German people. And from the start he had taken special pains with the young. Hitler had been in power only three months when, in April 1933, virtually all German clubs for boys and girls between the ages of 10 and 18 were consolidated by the state. Both sexes went into the Hitler Youth, but the girls' adjunct was called the League of German Girls.

Led in the prewar years by Baldur von Schirach, an ardent champion of Nazism, the young were set on a course of toughening themselves mentally and physically in the service of the Reich. They camped in Germany's abundant forests, helped harvest crops, and exercised in relentless unison. They also learned to parrot the gospel of Nazism:

> *You, Führer, are our commander!*
> *We stand in your name.*
> *The Reich is the object of our struggle,*
> *It is the beginning and the amen.*

Within a year, membership in the Hitler Youth had leaped to nearly 3.6 million; when war came in 1939, it had reached 8.9 million—and that did not include the millions who had outgrown the program and passed into the mainstream of German life. The graduates of the Hitler Youth never stopped fighting for Hitler's Germany, even when, after six years of war, the nation began crashing around them.

Exemplars of German womankind, members of an organization for girls over 17 known as the Faith and Beauty Corps perform a precision exercise.

"Führer command, we follow! All say 'Yes!' " reads the banner on a truck that carries Hitler Youths to a propaganda demonstration in Berlin in 1934.

LESSONS IN THE NAZI CREED

The Hitler Youth organization secured its grip on its members with a mixture of constant activity and a heady ideology designed to instill the proud belief that they belonged to a select community.

At least once a week every group held a session at which the tenets of Nazism were expounded. Texts approved by Nazi officials included exciting stories of war and such volumes as *The German Condition and Fate* and *People without Space*, which extolled the past and future greatness of the German people.

On occasion, to add spice to an evening, a leader might conduct his young charges in a raid against a neighboring Hitler Youth unit—just to show how invigorating combat could be.

Before an inscription glorifying struggle, girls of a Hitler Youth club follow their leader in song.

Seated underneath a model glider, a Hitler Youth group assembles for an evening of music and indoctrination around a table strewn with Nazi Party texts.

Ten young women balance with a rolling hoop at a national competition held in 1934. The girls' performances usually stressed grace and coordination.

A ZEST FOR HEALTH AND TEAMWORK

There was no question that brawn out-ranked brains in Nazi Germany. "Training of the intellectual faculties represents only a secondary aim," Hitler wrote. "A man of small intellectual attainment, but physically healthy, is more valuable to the national community than an educated weakling."

Hitler Youth programs therefore emphasized physical training—muscle building, cross-country hikes and combat games. Hours of drilling were capped by frequent field days and by competitions that engaged teams from all over the Reich. For winning teams, the reward sometimes was an audience with the Führer himself.

Conspicuously, the zeal for excellence focused on the group, not on the individual, for the goal was to develop a generation that would one day fight for Germany as a team. A Hitler Youth maxim put it this way: "Anything that undermines our unity must go on the pyre!"

Packing military field gear, Hitler Youths stride past timekeepers in a speed-hiking competition.

Human chariots—consisting of one boy mounted on the backs of two others and holding reins attached to three more—race at a Hitler Youth field day.

In an open-air classroom, Motor Hitler Youths study a diagram of a motorcycle engine. The boys were taught how to repair their vehicles on the road.

GAMES WITH A MILITARY CAST

The sports emphasized most by the Hitler Youth were those with a potential military application. From the start, youth groups trained and competed in navigating across country. They might be driven miles from their base camps and then have to return through unfamiliar territory in the dark.

By 1938 many Hitler Youth groups paralleled branches of the German armed forces. Some 62,000 youngsters of the Marine Hitler Youth participated in such activities as sailing down the Danube or in the Baltic aboard Naval training vessels. The Motor Hitler Youth, nearly 100,000 strong, modeled themselves after the motorized Storm Troopers, roaring about the countryside on motorcycles.

Still another 78,000 smartly uniformed lads belonged to the air branch of the Hitler Youth. They built model planes and gliders, earned flying certificates and enjoyed the special privilege of making frequent flights in the bombers and fighters of the reborn German Air Force.

Maneuvering their open boats in the North Sea, Marine Hitler Youths rig a sail and catch a breeze.

Strapped into a glider, an earnest youngster gets a takeoff push from boys behind. Germany later pioneered the use of gliders to transport troops.

An officer quizzes youngsters at a National Political Academy. The students, organized into "platoons," were taught to cultivate a "soldierly attitude."

SPECIAL SCHOOLING FOR FUTURE LEADERS

German boys and girls who showed particular promise qualified for admission to special schools. About 50 such schools trained them to become leaders of the Hitler Youth, and 31 National Political Academies—28 for boys and three for girls—trained the most outstanding youngsters, beginning at the age of 10, to be future leaders of the Reich itself. The academies were administered under a military regimen, and the curricula included not only traditional learning but also the political concerns of the state. Students were sent into mines and factories and were then required to write reports on how those institutions functioned.

Entrance competition was keen, and the screening rigorous; the typical National Political Academy received about 400 applications each year but admitted fewer than 30 students. The applicants first had to undergo scrutiny by academy teachers and physicians, then endure a week of tests. Some of the criteria of fitness were bizarre: One examination measured the candidate's skull to make sure that it was sufficiently "Aryan" in shape.

Parents had no right to prevent their children from attending the academies; one widow who demurred when a schoolmaster recommended her son for a special school received a sharp reply. "You had better adjust your ideas," she was told. "Your son is not your personal property. He is on loan to you but he is the property of the German people."

In a Potsdam park, girls training to become group leaders in the League of German Girls perform their morning exercises.

Deeply engrossed, Hitler Youth members read quietly in the library of their Berlin academy. All their books, from fairy tales to war histories, were censored.

BASIC TRAINING IN THE ARTS OF WAR

In the later 1930s, Hitler Youth training became even more conspicuously military. "We wish to reach the point," said one leader of the organization, "where the gun rests as securely as the pen in the hand of boys. It is a curious state of mind for a nation when for years it spends many hours a day on calligraphy, but not a single hour on shooting."

The Nazis set about to reverse that imbalance. By 1937 the Hitler Youth had its own rifle school, which during its first year taught 1.5 million boys how to shoot. At the beginning of the War, boys aged 15 and older went to special camps for three weeks of basic infantry training. Eventually even preteenagers were recruited to man antiaircraft defenses.

With few exceptions, the boys accepted their duty with resolution. "Rather than surrender," recalled an American officer who in 1945 faced an artillery unit of Hitler Youths, "the boys fought until they were killed." They had learned the lesson exemplified in their tenet: "We were born to die for Germany."

Using binoculars and a compass, a Hitler Youth team seeks out its objective during a test in map reading. From 1939 on, the German armed forces supervised

Singing as they go, Hitler Youth skiers march behind a corporal from an Army mountain unit.

all Hitler Youth marksmanship training and field exercises.

At a school in the Odenwald, a Hitler Youth class learns how to take apart and clean a rifle.

AN HONORED PLACE FOR YOUTH

Every September, Adolf Hitler treated the Germans to an immense extravaganza that served as a reminder of the glories of Nazism. The ritual began with journeys on foot and by train from every village and hamlet to the railhead city of Nuremberg. There a full week of festivities—games, exhibitions and speeches—culminated in a stirring oration by the Führer.

Invariably, the Hitler Youth played a prominent role. A British journalist who witnessed the first such rally in 1933 wrote that the youngsters were "breathtaking in their marvelous coordination." That year 60,000 boys marched into the stadium at Nuremberg, assembled in a formation that spelled out their motto, *Blut und Ehre*— "Blood and honor"—then separated and did it again. As a grand finale, all 60,000 drew sparkling daggers—symbolizing that the Reich was spoiling for a fight, and daring anyone to meet the challenge.

Bound for Nuremberg in 1938, flag bearers lead a group of Hitler Youth through the town of Fürth.

A tent city on the outskirts of Nuremberg houses Hitler Youth members during the week-long rally.

Three young trumpeters—each with a hand placed on his dagger hilt—look out at the flag-bedecked Nuremberg stadium and its tightly packed stands.

1

If ever there was an occasion that reflected the mystical and fateful union that existed between the Führer, Adolf Hitler, and the German people—and that sustained the nation through the travails of World War II—the spectacular evening ceremony of the 10th Nazi Party Congress on September 10, 1937, was such an event. Its combination of glorious pageantry and reassuring ritual evoked an outpouring of fervent emotion on both sides of the alliance. At the start, more than 140,000 Nazi Party officials of greater and lesser rank wheeled into Nuremberg's Zeppelin Field, precision-marching in 32 columns representing the 32 political districts in Hitler's Third Reich. Shouldering 32,000 party banners, the marchers suggested in their advance a magical sort of menace, like an autumnal forest on the move. One by one the columns passed the reviewing stand, on which stood Robert Ley, head of the German Labor Front. They then took their places on the grassy infield that stretched in front of the stand.

When the last of the columns had reached its place, Ley about-faced toward the rear of the stand, and as he did so Adolf Hitler strode on stage. Hand on belt buckle, he arrived at the rostrum and froze in a heroic pose, an icy statue dappled by the flickering of two ceremonial braziers at either end of the stand. Ley addressed him, welcoming him as the nation's leader to the annual gathering of party members in the name of German labor, to whom this year's rally was dedicated. Only then did Hitler stir. His chin shot out and, as it did, 150 antiaircraft searchlights thrust columns of light heavenward. Hitting low clouds overhead, their beams diffused, bathing the entire field in a flat luminescence. A quarter of a million voices shouting *"Sieg heil!"* echoed in the night.

Hitler spoke into a bank of microphones before him—addressing not only those who were present, but an unseen audience of millions who crowded around their living-room radios throughout the land. Taking the attitude of a bridegroom addressing his bride—an image he frequently invoked—Hitler pledged his troth to the German people. "You have found me," he cried in a spirit of gladness. "You have believed in me. This has given your life a new meaning, a new mission." Had he wanted, he could have enumerated all the rich gifts that in the past four years he had bestowed on the bride as a token of his love—a remilitar-

"ONE PEOPLE, ONE LEADER!"

ized Rhineland, five million jobs for workers, higher prices for farmers, a gross national product up 102 per cent, and an Army, a Navy and an Air Force to quicken the pride and preserve the safety of all.

But Hitler did not dwell on those matters. Instead, he pledged for the future that he and the German *Volk,* or common people, would "stand as the skirmish line of the nation," thereby suggesting that Germany stood united and ready to fight a hostile world. For a moment he paused. Then, as he resumed, Hitler took on the tone of soliloquy. "Finding you," he breathed into the bank of microphones, "is what made my life's struggle possible."

In concluding, Hitler thrust his arm forward in a gesture that had become known as "the German greeting" and exclaimed *"Deutschland, Sieg heil!"* The massed audience responded jubilantly *"Heil Hitler!"* and sang the stirring national anthem, "Deutschland, Deutschland über Alles" —"Germany, Germany over All." The sound, noted an official account, was "organ-like," and when the 150 searchlights switched aim and intersected overhead, the effect was "cathedral-like."

Thus concluded what might be called the nuptials of *Volk* and *Führer*—people and leader—a marriage that was to hold them together, for better or for worse, through the grim years ahead.

To be sure, many a German witness to the occasion might have taken a more straightforward view of the events on that September evening in 1937. But the image of wedlock between *Volk* and *Führer* was Hitler's own, and it had some metaphoric truth. Like most marriages, this one began with faith, hope and promises for a bright future. It continued through a honeymoon of heady exhilaration and material acquisitions, and settled into a life that would withstand any number of disappointments and disillusionments before it was rent asunder.

If finding the German people had made his life worthwhile, as Hitler so dramatically professed, the Germans by and large reciprocated the feeling. Wherever Hitler went, he was greeted by mass demonstrations that often bordered on hysteria. His devotees covered a broad spectrum, from the exiled Kaiser's son, Crown Prince Friedrich Wilhelm, who publicly endorsed Hitler, to little children who said a prayer for "our Führer" before they went to sleep at night.

To millions of Germans it seemed that Hitler, in his role as husband, had provided both the spiritual and material well-being they had previously been denied.

The Germans were a despondent people when Hitler first undertook to lead them in the early 1930s. The middle class was in tatters, farmers were drowning in debt, laborers were out of work, many aristocratic landowners were impoverished, and industrial magnates were glumly presiding over an output that had shrunk to less than half of what it had been in 1929, before the world was plunged into the Great Depression.

Germany indeed had never recovered from World War I, which had cost the nation 1.8 million of its fighting men. The ravages of that conflict had been followed by what most Germans regarded as humiliating and iniquitous terms of peace. The $33 billion in reparations payments levied on them under the treaty signed at Versailles seemed impossibly high. The seizure of territories dictated at Versailles also seemed unfair. The coal-rich Saar, German in both speech and sentiment, was ceded to France for 15 years of exploitation. Alsace-Lorraine, which was ceded permanently to France, had as many German ties as French. A corridor of land given to the Poles cut off East Prussia from the rest of Germany. The Baltic port of Danzig at the corridor's northern end became a free city administered by the League of Nations.

To these grievances, the Versailles Treaty added yet another: Germany, a nation that had considered the Army one of its proudest ornaments and industrial production one of its greatest strengths, was restricted to a token armed force of only 100,000 men and was forbidden to build heavy armaments—leaving the nation defenseless in an unfriendly world.

One of the consequences of the passions aroused by these seemingly insoluble grievances was that the politics of Germany fragmented during the 1920s. By the end of the decade as many as 28 parties sat in the Reichstag, the parliamentary body that represented the 32 voting districts in Germany and a 33rd comprising Germans who lived outside the borders of the Reich. In 1930 ten of those parties had polled more than one million votes apiece. No party had a majority, and all were working at cross-purposes. The

two most conspicuous parties were the Communists, who championed the workers at the expense of both capitalism and nationalism, and the National Socialist German Workers' Party—the Nazis—who also spoke out for the workers, yet managed to interest the Army and the industrialists as well, by appealing to their nationalistic yearnings for a greater Germany.

Other parties represented the monarchists, who longed for a restoration of the Kaiser; the rank and file of World War I soldiers, who felt cheated; the aristocratic landholders; the small shopkeepers; and the farmers. In some instances, the interests of economics and class were further confused by age-old concerns of geography and tradition. In the mind of many an aristocrat, for instance, being a Prussian or a Bavarian counted for more than being a German.

So bitter was the bickering among the various parties that the Reichstag was paralyzed. It sometimes happened that if government was to operate at all, the President had to invoke a clause in the Constitution that authorized him to suspend civil liberties and rule by decree. But the potential danger of that expedient caused little concern. The very paralysis of the Reichstag had done much to discredit the principle of parliamentary democracy in the eyes of many Germans, and if there was one matter on which they could agree it was that the republic that had emerged from World War I was a failure, and in dire need of reform.

For the average German, of graver concern than such political troubles were the economic ones. In the early 1920s inflation swept the land; the value of the reichsmark plummeted disastrously, wiping out virtually all cash savings, pensions and investments in insurance. For a time, Germans literally needed wheelbarrows of money to do their shopping. A brief period of stability in the late 1920s was interrupted by the reversals that plunged the entire world into an unprecedented economic depression.

In Germany the Depression created six million unemployed in a working population of 29 million. The middle and working classes alike were ruined. In the better neighborhoods of towns throughout Germany, formerly well-starched bureaucrats and businessmen could be seen slinking around in frayed clothing. In the working-class districts, men who had formerly been industrious and self-assured

Blazing antiaircraft searchlights surround Storm Troopers at the annual Nuremberg Rally. "The Nuremberg meetings," wrote correspondent William L. Shirer, "had something of the mysticism and religious fervor of an Easter or Christmas Mass in a great Gothic cathedral."

now spent listless days at their neighborhood beer halls. In front of them the tables were bare; an unemployed man living on a government dole of 16 reichsmarks a month—reduced to seven, after the first year—could not afford 50 pfennigs for a beer.

In the German countryside, thousands of farms were idle and foreclosed; the farmers were in debt by 12 billion marks and saddled with 14 per cent interest rates that they could not pay.

The glories of the German past perversely underscored the anguish of the present. What had happened to a people who had once been so proud—so extraordinarily well educated, talented in the arts, endowed in the natural sciences, industrious, enterprising, martial, disciplined? Other nations had experienced hard times in the aftermath of World War I and with the onset of the Depression, but other peoples had somehow muddled through. In Germany, desperation hung in the air.

Onto the national stage of that stricken land came Adolf Hitler, lawfully appointed Chancellor of the German Reich in January 1933. "One state, one people, one leader!" he cried in a pledge to bring unity to the fractured nation—at the same time making a special appeal to each of the nation's interest groups. To the Army he promised a return of military prowess, to the captains of industry and the aristocratic landholders a restoration of the economy, to the laborers work, to youth a role in carrying out the destiny of a Reich that would endure for 1,000 years. So doing, Adolf Hitler took charge of a people that had been leaderless and adrift. He gave hope to a nation in despair, pride to a nation humiliated.

Hitler's rise to public office coincided with the phenomenal growth of the party whose standard he bore. When he joined it in 1919, the infant German Workers' Party had only 54 members, a pitiful treasury of 7 marks, 50 pfennigs, and headquarters in a dingy room at the rear of a Munich beer hall. Hitler gave the party a new name—and a new leader. By exercising a talent for galvanizing people into political action and a genius for public speaking, Hitler rapidly built the National Socialists into the most formidable political bloc in the politically splintered nation. In the elections of July 1932, the Nazis polled 13.7 million votes and won 230 of the Parliament's 608 seats—not a majority, but the largest representation in the Reichstag.

More significant for the events that followed was the fact that the election success ultimately earned the Nazis three positions in the German Cabinet in January 1933. Chief among the posts was that of Chancellor, which Adolf Hitler won for himself by striking a temporary accommodation with the conservatives in the Reichstag. As Chancellor, Hitler was the Cabinet's ranking member, second in power only to Germany's elected President, Paul von Hindenburg. And Hindenburg, at 86, was physically frail and was becoming senile.

One of the other two posts that went to Nazis was Minister of the Interior, a department with a broad franchise to influence such vital areas of daily life as schools and internal security; it went to Wilhelm Frick, a career civil servant who had been a close associate of Hitler's for most of the party's brief history. The other post went to Hermann Göring, a flamboyant figure who had won celebrity as a fighter pilot during World War I. For the time being there was no special responsibility for Göring; he was named minister without portfolio and was promised that he would become Minister of Aviation as soon as Germany was able to build an air force.

With these few but vital posts at their command, Hitler

Spanning two walls, a dramatic mural showing an outsized Hitler among Germany's working masses provides a backdrop for a Berlin exhibit in 1937. One observer called such events "masterpieces of theatrical art."

and his fellow Nazis acted swiftly to deliver on their campaign promises. They froze prices at Depression levels in order to stem a renewed inflation. They began massive rearmament, thus obliging both the Army and the industrialists and providing jobs for millions of unemployed laborers as well. They inaugurated grand public works, thus providing not only employment for the men who built them but manifest evidence for the rest of the nation that something exciting was afoot. One such project was a four-lane highway system known as the *Autobahn*. A precursor of the modern freeway, the autobahn eventually snaked its way 2,000 miles through the heart of Germany and allowed drivers to travel for hundreds of miles at a stretch at the novel speed of 50 miles per hour. The highway system was one that the ordinary citizen could aspire to use once he had a car—and Hitler soon promised cars for every working family *(page 29)*.

The results of these Nazi innovations were dynamic. In one year, unemployment was reduced by half, to three million; in 1937 it was down to 1.1 million, and by 1938 instead of unemployment Germany had a shortage of labor. Meanwhile, planes, tanks and artillery pieces rolled off German assembly lines by the thousands, along with high-quality cameras and toys. A government-supported building boom saw the construction of monumental public edifices, sports arenas and homes for German workers.

All these advances were made at considerable cost in human freedoms. The major losers were the Jews, longstanding targets of Hitler's enmity and the alleged obstacle to his design for a new Germany. As early as April 1933, Jews were excluded from holding public office, from working in the civil service, and from several professions, including teaching and journalism. With the promulgation of the Nuremberg laws of September 1935 they were denied citizenship and the vote, and were forbidden to marry Aryans. By 1938 they were eliminated from the fields of law and medicine.

Jews were not the only ones to endure constraints; within six months of taking power Hitler had abolished the myriad political parties, and from then on anyone who expressed dissatisfaction with the regime was likely to be questioned, or worse, by the police. But Germans made few objections; they were glad to have work and self-respect once more. "We loved the fatherland," wrote Inge Scholl, who was then a high-school student in Ulm. "And Hitler, so we heard on all sides, would help the fatherland achieve greatness, happiness and prosperity and ensure that everyone had work and bread. He would not rest until every German was free and happy." In that spirit most Germans shrugged and accepted, if they noticed at all, the constraints that accompanied the great advances that Hitler brought them.

Not the least of the reasons underlying Hitler's success was an uncanny ability to seize on incidents—nothing was too small to warrant his notice—and exploit them to the hilt. On the night of February 27, just one month after he had become Chancellor, the Reichstag building in Berlin went up in flames. On the scene the police found a mentally retarded man, and known pyromaniac, named Marinus van der Lübbe, whom they arrested and charged with the deed. Hitler's colleague Hermann Göring now had charge of the Prussian police force. That same night, Göring had his men arrest 4,000 Communists and other political antagonists of the Nazis. They were accused of complicity in setting the fire, and clapped into prison.

The next day, Chancellor Hitler went to President von Hindenburg and gave a highly colored account of the fire, suggesting that van der Lübbe had acted in collusion with

Hitler officiates at the opening of the Frankfurt-to-Darmstadt stretch of the autobahn in May 1935. Between 1933 and 1938, workers added 2,000 miles to the "highways of the Führer," a road network actually begun in 1928.

the Communists. Indicating that the safety of the nation was at stake unless stern measures were taken, Hitler persuaded Hindenburg to sign a decree "for the protection of the people and state." The decree nullified the right of habeas corpus, thus giving the police the right to arrest any person or group without due process of law.

A few hours later came a second decree that Hitler promoted as a safeguard "against betrayal of the German people and treasonous machinations." It replaced constitutional government with what amounted to a permanent state of emergency.

The two decrees, while purporting to defend the nation against insidious elements that sought to overthrow the government, in fact signaled the end of individual liberties for all Germans. From then on, police were empowered to open letters, monitor telephone calls, examine bank accounts, and search property and persons without a warrant.

Within a month came another measure that secured Hitler's grasp on the government. On March 23, the Nazis forced through the Reichstag legislation entitled Law for the Removal of the Distress of People and Reich. It was popularly and accurately called the Enabling Act, for it passed control of the government from the Reichstag to the executive branch, enabling Hitler and his fellow Nazis to direct affairs of state without consulting the Reichstag at all. "A historic day," crowed the party newspaper *Völkischer Beobachter, (People's Observer).* "The parliamentary system has capitulated to the new Germany."

Indeed it had. From now on Germany would be ruled by decree alone. Thus armed, the Nazis moved to infiltrate—and control—every area of German life. The party had a word for it, *Gleichschaltung*—"putting everything in the same gear." The first decree that Hitler promulgated under the Enabling Act dissolved virtually all of the provincial assemblies that regulated local affairs for the 32 voting districts. It gave Hitler the right to name the district governors, who thenceforth answered directly to him. The Enabling Act was soon invoked for two other decrees of much grimmer consequence. One established concentration camps for holding "in protective custody" all persons whom the Nazis deemed "harmful to the people." Within a year 50 such camps had sprung up, from Prussia in the north to Bavaria in the south—and 27,000 persons were already interned in

them. The other decree enlarged from three to 46 the number of crimes punishable by death; among them were arson, unauthorized demonstrations and attacks on members of the government.

All these moves Hitler had made within the lawful limits of his post as Chancellor. Then on August 2, 1934, President von Hindenburg died. Hitler took over Hindenburg's functions as President; he swiftly discarded that title, continuing to style himself Chancellor, and added a new one: Führer of the Reich. He called for a plebiscite to approve his concentration of power, and 90 per cent of the voters—38 million of them—voted "Yes."

It was not surprising that they did. To a people accustomed for more than a decade to ineffectual parliamentary rule, the curtailment of democratic institutions seemed of little significance. Moreover, throughout the year and a half that Hitler was consolidating his power, he had spared no effort to woo the people on matters that affected them directly and personally.

High on Hitler's list of concerns was Germany's frustrated work force. He had been in office only four months when he declared May Day, the traditional day of celebration for workers, a national holiday and issued a slogan for it: "Honor work and respect the worker." Throughout the land working men and women were given the day off to celebrate at picnics and rallies; their union leaders were flown to Tempelhof airfield in Berlin to attend a rally that Hitler himself addressed. The very next day he moved to bring the previously independent unions under his thumb. He amalgamated them into one comprehensive organization that he called the German Labor Front. In charge of it he appointed Robert Ley, a chemist from Cologne and an ardent Nazi.

Ley went right to work subverting the old union system. Portraying himself as a "poor peasant's son who understands poverty and the exploitation of anonymous capitalism," he promised work for all, and proclaimed that employers could no longer arbitrarily fire a worker. There were several hidden drawbacks, however, to these guarantees. One was that no worker could leave a job without the government's permission, and only the state employment offices could arrange a new job for him.

THE PROMISE OF A "PEOPLE'S CAR"

Not least of the ways Hitler won over the German people was by promising worldly goods for all. At the Berlin Automobile Show in 1934, he announced that designer Ferdinand Porsche had drawn up plans for a *Volkswagen,* or ''people's car''—and that the vehicle would be made available to citizens of even modest means.

At a time when only one German in 100 owned an automobile, Hitler's announcement was revolutionary. He proposed a layaway plan: For five marks per week, any German could buy government-issued savings stamps over a four-year period toward the purchase of one of Porsche's glossy black, beetle-shaped little cars.

Spurred by an advertising campaign that included the poster at left, 336,668 Germans invested 280 million marks in the plan. But by 1939 only 210 VWs had been built—and most of them went to Nazi officials. Then Hitler's plan for civilian cars was scrapped as the unfinished Volkswagen plant turned to war production.

Porsche's design was adapted into two military versions. One, the *Kübelwagen,* was a cross-country vehicle similar to the American jeep, but it lacked four-wheel drive. It weighed only 1,100 pounds, making it easy to push out of ditches and bogs. The other was the amphibious *Schwimmwagen (below),* which featured a retractable propeller and a machine-gun mounting on the passenger side.

The 280 million marks ended up in the pockets of the Nazis' bitterest enemies: The Russians seized it from a Berlin bank at the end of the War. The Volkswagen company, however, returned to civilian production in late 1945—and 35 years later was still honoring the savings stamps presented by German citizens.

Attended by Ferry Porsche (left), son of the designer, and by SS officials, Hitler inspects one of the 15,000 amphibious Volkswagens produced in wartime.

To assuage employers, Ley and the Nazi government abolished collective bargaining and declared strikes illegal. Later they abolished the limitations—hard won by the unions—on the number of hours a person could be made to work. Eventually, Germans found themselves working 60 to 72 hours a week. In effect, job security had become a kind of bondage.

Few German workers grumbled, however. By 1936, the average factory worker was earning 35 marks a week—almost 10 times more than the unemployment compensation of 1932. Taxes and obligatory contributions to the party sliced between 15 and 35 per cent from the total, but such deductions seemed a small price to pay for the security of work and the guarantee of respectable support for the workers' families.

Labor chieftain Ley liked to preach that "it is more important to feed the souls of men than their stomachs," and in that spirit Hitler's government set out to provide more than the food that basic wages would buy. It zealously courted the working class by enlivening its leisure time. A government program called "Strength through Joy" bombarded workers with an astonishing variety of adult-education courses, music recitals, sports events and theater performances, all available at low cost. If the inexpensive tickets were not actually a bargain—the cost was deducted from the pay of all workers, regardless of whether or not they wished to participate—the fact was scarcely noticed. By the late 1930s, the Strength-through-Joy program had 25 million members.

One of the most popular of its offerings was the subsidized vacation. For 28 marks—or less than a typical week's wages—a worker could spend a week in the Harz Mountains; for 155 marks, or approximately a month's pay, he could tour Italy. The program also offered a lucky few, chosen for their hard work and party loyalty, a cruise on one of several ocean liners built especially for the purpose. In 1938 alone, 180,000 workers and their families went on such cruises.

The Strength-through-Joy program, seductive in itself, was enhanced by a subtle suggestion that Nazism was abolishing class distinctions. On the cruises, all passengers regardless of status drew lots for their cabin accommodations. The implication was reinforced in other ways: The Nazis contended that they were uniting "work of the head and the hand," and on May Day, 1934, a factory worker and the rector of the prestigious University of Heidelberg rode together through the streets of Heidelberg atop a brightly decorated beer wagon. "The worker," said Robert Ley, "sees that we are serious about raising his social position." Germany's controlled press informed readers that garbage

Participants in a Strength-through-Joy tour pause at a Rhine valley overlook. In 1938, six million workers, one out of every five in Germany, enjoyed a trip as part of the Nazis' organized leisure program.

collectors belonged to a "peerage of hard jobs," that "barbers face great tasks," and that Hitler himself had once been a construction worker.

Even the freewheeling machine that Hitler's Minister of Propaganda, Joseph Goebbels, set up could not turn the Führer into a German farmer, but it did try to make farmers feel important by describing them as the roots of a new nobility based on blood and soil. The Nazi Party took control of Germany's farmers as it had taken control of trade union members: by making new guarantees in place of old problems, and by replacing existing organizations with others of their own design. In October 1933 the Nazi-controlled

Reichstag designated all farms smaller than 300 acres "hereditary farms," and the men who owned them "hereditary farmers." Such farms, which constituted about one third of the three million in Germany, could neither be sold by their owners nor foreclosed by creditors; the new law also set a limit on the debt that farm owners had to repay. To those thousands of farmers who were already heavily in debt and who despaired of meeting the payments they already owed, such a measure seemed heaven-sent.

At the same time, Hitler's government abolished two old agricultural organizations, the Union of Christian Peasants and the Association of Agricultural Communities. All farming enterprise was thenceforth answerable to a newly ap-

From a gunboat at dockside, Hitler sees off a cruise ship—one of six that carried more than 7,000 vacationers to the Norwegian fjords in 1937. The Strength-through-Joy program eventually subsidized every kind of social activity, from concerts to folk dancing.

pointed administrator, Walter Darré, a pig farmer and loyal Nazi who was anointed Reich Peasant Leader and Minister of Food and Agriculture.

Darré and the Nazis made much ado about the Hereditary Farm Law and the security it bestowed upon the German farmer. But, like the labor laws, it had hidden drawbacks. While precluding the sale or foreclosure of a farm, the law bound the hereditary farmer to the land, and obliged him to produce government-dictated crops and sell them at government-dictated prices. Under the old law of primogeniture, which was not abolished, the farmer's eldest son was equally bound. Another drawback was that while promising to keep the farmer out of debt, the law limited the credit available to him. That stricture put the small farmers—65 per cent of whose properties lacked even such conveniences as running water—at a disadvantage. The great landholders, who were not restricted in the amount of money they could borrow, quickly went about modernizing their farms.

The credit restrictions gave hereditary farmers another problem; they were unable to hire the extra hands they needed at planting and harvest times. The Nazis had a solution to that, however—one that reaped double benefits to the party. They conscripted boys between the ages of 14 and 18, and young women between 17 and 25, for one year's service on the farms. Thus the farms were tended and Germany's young people received a healthy tour of outdoor life, as well as a heady feeling that they were helping to serve the fatherland.

Hitler made no secret of the fact that he was depending on "his" children to make the dream of the Thousand-Year Reich a reality. "When an opponent declares, 'I will not come over to your side,'" he said in November 1933, "I

calmly say, 'Your child already belongs to us. What are you? You will pass on. Your descendants, however, now stand in the new camp. In a short time they will know nothing else but this new community.'"

Hitler had begun wooing the youth long before he became Chancellor. In 1926, as the leader of a Nazi Party still struggling to establish itself, he approved the founding of a special unit of the party to be called the *Hitler Jugend,* or Hitler Youth. In 1931 he put in charge of it an ebullient young follower named Baldur von Schirach.

Schirach was a good choice. At 21 he was young enough to be not far removed from his charges; as the son of an aristocratic family, he had been brought up in the tradition of military leadership. (His mother was American and his great-grandfather a Union officer who had lost a leg in the Civil War.)

Shortly after the Nazis came to power, Schirach proved his political mettle. On April 3, 1933, he had 50 members of the Hitler Youth march to the Berlin office of the government bureau that registered Germany's miscellaneous boys' and girls' clubs. The young Nazis occupied the bureau and commandeered the office staff. The coup gave Schirach effective control of files that told him everything he could want to know about six million German youngsters—their ages, backgrounds, interests and aptitudes, from religious discussion to band-playing, from stamp-collecting to climbing mountains. At the time of the coup, membership in the Hitler Youth stood at little more than 100,000. A year later nearly three million young people were marching under the swastika banner.

Every village had its unit of the Hitler Youth; every city and province had several. Members of the Hitler Youth retained their special interests, and they engaged in spirited competition with one another. "Every unit wanted to have

Wielding their spades with military precision, members of the National Labor Service perform at a 1935 rally in Anhalt. Up to 100,000 workers marched in such parades to prove the Nazis' ability to harness manpower.

the most interesting expedition log and the biggest collection for the Winter Relief Fund," recalled Melita Maschmann, a leader of a girls' branch of the Hitler Youth. "In the musical competitions, Hitler Youth choirs, fife and drum bands, chamber orchestras and amateur theatrical groups competed for the glory of the most brilliant performance." Significantly, all of this was done in a spirit of serving Adolf Hitler. "Your name, my Führer, is the happiness of youth; your name, my Führer, is for us everlasting life," was typical of the pseudoreligious refrains that were spouted at German children by the cadre of young men and women—most of them in their twenties—whom Schirach installed as leaders of the Hitler Youth.

This identification with the Führer imbued millions of German children with the feeling that they were helping Hitler to restore Germany's pride and to build a new nation. "Germans began to hold up their heads again," Melita Maschmann recalled. "At last Germany was no longer the plaything of her enemies. I continued to go to school, but service in the Hitler Youth took up every free minute. I was obsessed by the vision of a Greater German Empire. Previous empires had been built up in the course of many generations. We would surpass them all in the twinkling of an eye. I did not allow myself an hour of rest." Within a few years Baldur von Schirach could boast without exaggeration: "I have educated this generation in the belief of and in faithfulness to Hitler."

Not surprisingly, the Nazis also took over the schools—from kindergarten up. Even the littlest schoolchild's day began with the Hitler salute, in accordance with a protocol laid down by Interior Minister Frick in December 1934. "At the beginning of each lesson," he ordered, "the teacher goes in front of the class, which is standing, and greets it by raising his right arm and with the words 'Heil Hitler!' The class returns the salute by raising their right arms, and with the words 'Heil Hitler!' "

The school day progressed in the same manner. Nazi theory pervaded books on all kinds of subjects—even fairy tales. The story of Cinderella became an epic struggle between a racially pure German maiden and her alien stepmother. Cinderella is rescued from her dismal lot because the prince—also a racially pure German—is guided by "the voice of blood," or racial instinct. In biology courses, German students learned that such traits as their blue eyes and blond hair meant they were Aryan—a racial stock "superior" to the Slavs in neighboring lands, and to the Jews at home. In history classes, they were taught that there was a line of continuity running from Charlemagne to Frederick the Great to Adolf Hitler, thus putting the Führer in the pantheon of Germany's greatest heroes. Geography lessons emphasized the German need for more "living space"—thus justifying the series of territorial acquisitions that Hitler launched in 1938, when he annexed Austria to the Reich.

Even arithmetic lessons were couched in terms that drove home Nazi-sanctioned race consciousness. One question in an elementary-school textbook asked, "How many children must a family produce in order to secure the quantitative continuance of the German people?" The answer, according to Hitler himself, was four. Another problem subtly conditioned children to scorn "undesirable" citizens and by extension to approve—no matter whether they understood it—a program of euthanasia that the government quietly introduced in 1939. "A mentally handicapped person costs the public four reichsmarks a day, a cripple 5.5 reichsmarks and a convicted criminal 3.5 reichsmarks," read the problem. "Cautious estimates state that within the bounds of the German Reich, 300,000 persons are being cared for in pub-

Eager youngsters dressed in their Hitler Youth uniforms peer through the legs of SS men at a 1935 parade in Berlin. "A holy shiver ran down our spines," one youth later said, at the prospect of seeing the "beloved Führer."

CAUSTIC POSTERS THAT SATIRIZED THE NAZIS

Using a pair of scissors and a pot of paste, John Heartfield, a German Communist, converted pro-Nazi propaganda into brutal satires that debunked the dogmas of the Third Reich. Heartfield clipped photographs from published sources, including party newspapers, then reassembled the components with surprising results: The Christian Cross became a burdensome swastika, and Hitler turned into a leering butcher and a money-gulping glutton.

Before the Nazis came to power, Heartfield's incisive caricatures were featured in the *Arbeiter—Illustrierte Zeitung*, a Berlin-based leftist weekly with a circulation of more than 100,000 in Germany, Austria, Switzerland and Holland. Inevitably, as soon as Hitler became Chancellor, Heartfield was targeted for arrest. On the 16th of April, 1933, as secret police gathered in the street below his apartment, he crawled out a back window and fled to Prague, where he joined members of the *Arbeiter* staff who had already left Germany.

Over the next five years he continued his work for the journal, which was smuggled into Germany by the anti-Nazi underground. In 1938, when the Germans marched into Czechoslovakia, Heartfield took refuge in London, where he spent most of the war years.

Even from afar, Heartfield bedeviled the Nazis. They revoked his citizenship and banned his art work, but at least one attempt to censure his compositions backfired. When an SS newspaper published a selection of his montages in a scornful article, the public demand for the issue so alarmed SS leader Heinrich Himmler that he ordered all copies of the edition confiscated and burned.

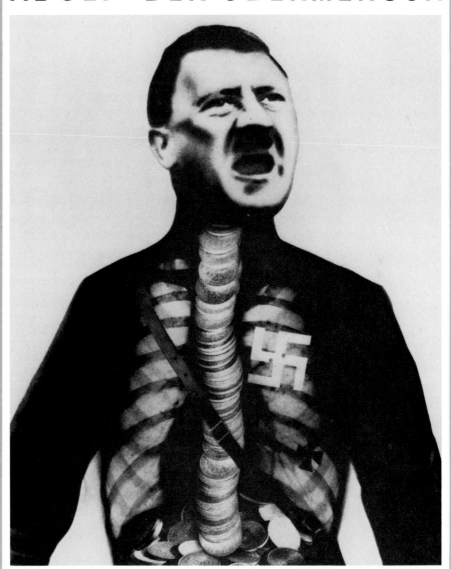

ADOLF – DER ÜBERMENSCH

SCHLUCKT GOLD UND REDET BLECH

His gullet crammed with coins, Hitler is cast as the bellicose spokesman of the rich in this 1932 montage captioned: "Adolf the superman swallows gold and spouts junk." At that time, caricaturist Heartfield believed the Führer was a capitalist bent on exploiting German workers.

Das Kreuz war noch nicht schwer genug

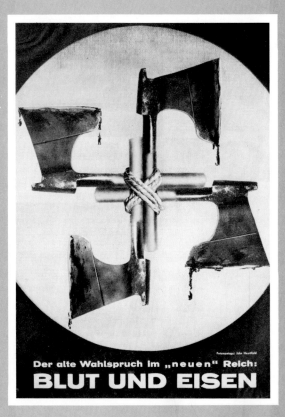

Der alte Wahlspruch im „neuen" Reich:
BLUT UND EISEN

With hammer and nails, a Nazi underling transforms the Cross of Christ into a swastika. The pictorial message is underscored by the words: "The Cross was not heavy enough."

NUR KEINE ANGST — ER IST VEGETARIER

Honing a fine edge on a butcher's knife, a blood-soiled Hitler prepares to dispatch a rooster wearing the liberty cap of France. The irony of the legend on this 1936 montage—"Don't worry, he's a vegetarian"— became clear four years later, when Germany devoured France.

This gory swastika fashioned from executioner's axes is labeled "Blood and iron," the motto of Otto von Bismarck, the belligerent 19th Century Chancellor who unified modern Germany.

lic mental institutions. How many marriage loans at 1,000 reichsmarks per couple could be financed annually from the funds allocated to institutions?'' The answer took time to calculate, but the implication was immediately clear.

By the time a graduate of the Nazi school system reached university level, he was not surprised to find Nazi dogma pervading his books and classrooms even there. When a veterinarian and fervent Nazi named Eugen Fischer became Rector of the University of Berlin in 1933, he immediately introduced to the curriculum 86 courses on veterinary medicine and another 25 courses on Nazi ''racial science,'' which taught that Aryans were superior to all other races.

If the Nazis' meddling with education had the desired effect of breeding a generation of obedient subjects, it had a disastrous effect on German universities—some of which were the oldest and most prestigious in Europe. During the first five years of the Nazi regime, nearly 30 per cent of all university professors left the country. Some of them—including many Jews—were evicted by Nazi purges; others chose to leave of their own accord rather than bend to Nazi dicta. Among the losses to Germany were some brilliant men and women who enhanced immeasurably the intellectual life of the nations to which they fled; they included the scientist Albert Einstein, physicist Lise Meitner, novelist Thomas Mann, psychiatrist Sigmund Freud and his daughter Anna, poet-dramatist Bertolt Brecht and architects Walter Gropius and Marcel Breuer.

Although enrollment at German universities dropped precipitously—in some cases, by more than 50 per cent—the Nazis took a cavalier approach to the flight of some of the nation's best minds. In a speech in 1938, Julius Streicher, Gauleiter of Franconia, summed up the Nazi attitude toward academics by sarcastically asking, ''If one put the brains of all university professors onto one side of a scale and the brain of the Führer onto the other, which side do you think would sink?'' In Hitler's view, the goal of education was not to prepare youth for the universities, but to prepare them for the National Labor Service and the Wehrmacht, Germany's armed forces.

Hitler had as little regard for religion as he had for higher education. Nevertheless he was at great pains to flatter the clergy—while working insistently to bring them under his

aegis. On July 20, 1933, Germany signed a treaty with the Vatican that guaranteed German Catholics freedom of religion and assured the Catholic Church in Germany the right to manage its own affairs. The pact gave Hitler the respectability of foreign acknowledgment—the Vatican was the first foreign state to recognize the nascent Nazi regime—and cost him only some vague promises. In return, he secured a vow that Catholic priests would refrain from engaging in German politics, and that foreign-born priests would hold no important posts in German Catholic organizations. For the Church that meant no sacrifice, as priests were not accustomed to becoming openly involved in politics; for Hitler it underscored his nationalistic policy, that Germany was for Germans.

Local officials zealous in their practice of Nazism, however, little honored the treaty's guarantees for freedom of religious practice. In some areas, children were prohibited from making the sign of the Cross in school—Göring proclaimed that the stiff-armed Nazi salute should be ''the only salute to Jesus Christ.'' In other areas religious art was ordered removed from walls.

Inevitably, clergymen began to chafe. A conference of Catholic bishops in 1935 published a letter attacking the Nazis for waging a ''war of annihilation'' against religion. The government countered with a law forbidding clergymen to speak out ''against the interests of the state.''

With Protestants, who had no spiritual leader abroad and a scattering of more than 30 different denominations at home, Hitler began on a different tack. In July 1933 he ordered all Protestant denominations lumped together as the German Christian Church. To head the new organization Hitler chose Ludwig Müller, a former Army chaplain and ardent nationalist on whom he bestowed the grand title Reich Bishop.

Most of the faithful went along without demur. In November of 1933, when 20,000 German Christians convened at the Sports Palace in Berlin, they overwhelmingly approved a number of far-reaching resolutions that insinuated Nazi dogma into Christian doctrine. One resolution rejected the entire Old Testament as a ''book for Jewish cattle''; another denied church membership to Jewish converts; a third deleted the writings of Saint Paul from the New Testament on the grounds that he was a ''Jew rabbi.'' Before long, echoing the Nazi slogan "One state, one people, one leader," Reich Bishop Müller was pronouncing "One state, one people, one church." The Nazi takeover of German Protestantism seemed complete.

Not quite. Here and there small but insistent voices of dissent began to be heard. One with which the Nazis would have to reckon came from Martin Niemöller, a minister of the Evangelical Church.

Niemöller, a small man who spoke in the clipped tones of a Prussian officer, was a former U-boat commander who had won celebrity for scuttling his boat at the close of World War I rather than let it pass into Allied hands. After the War

Niemöller entered the ministry and in 1934 he returned to the public eye when he published a book, *From U-Boat to Pulpit,* that became a bestseller. In the book, he gave Nazism a warm welcome, expressing the hope that the Nazis would be the avatar of a "national revival" from the "years of darkness" Germans had endured since 1918.

But the rapid inroads of Nazism into religious freedom soon gave Niemöller pause, and within a few months he reversed his position. Specifically, he balked at the official Church's adoption of anti-Semitism; more generally, he concluded that the goal of the Nazi program was to do away with Christianity altogether and replace religious teaching with what Hermann Göring called "the primeval voices of our race." Rallying a number of other Protestant ministers to his views, Niemöller established an organization he called the Pastors Emergency League. Overnight he attracted 1,300 followers; in three months he had 6,000. In March 1935 he held a synod, the result of which was a declaration denouncing the new Nazi paganism. The clergymen left the synod promising to disseminate the declaration in their parishes.

When the Ministry of the Interior learned of the synod's proclamation it forbade the reading of the document in public, but a number of ministers chose to disobey, and in March 1935 the Nazis summarily jailed more than 500 of them. Niemöller, protected for the moment by his celebrity, was not one of those arrested.

In May 1936 Niemöller grew bolder yet; he led his fellow pastors in sending a letter to Hitler denouncing anti-Semitism and protesting the religious doctrines that the state was imposing on the people. Hitler's answer was to arrest several hundred of Niemöller's followers. On June 27, 1937, Niemöller made still another public protest, this time from the pulpit of his church in Berlin. "No more will we keep silent; God commands us to speak," he declared. "One must obey God rather than men."

With this disavowal of Nazi primacy, Niemöller had gone too far. The police arrested him four days later and clapped him into prison, where he was subjected to several months of intense interrogation. Immediately upon his release in March of 1938, the Gestapo seized him and sent him to a concentration camp. Because of his national reputation, Niemöller was treated as a "special prisoner," but to make

Pastor Martin Niemöller, shown in a prewar photo, was placed in solitary confinement at Sachsenhausen and Dachau for denouncing the Nazis from the pulpit of his Berlin church. A U-boat commander during the First World War, Niemöller asked his captors for a U-boat command at the outset of World War II, hoping to continue his anti-Nazi campaign clandestinely once he had been set free.

sure he caused no further trouble he was put in solitary confinement, where he remained throughout the War. After Niemöller's imprisonment, most clergymen in Germany, whatever their faith, retreated to the safer course of limiting their remarks to religious doctrine, and abstained from offering political opinions.

All of Germany—and much of the rest of the world—eventually learned of the Reverend Niemöller's imprisonment. Less well known was the fact that many ordinary citizens had suffered a similar punishment, or worse. All told, an astonishing 225,000 Germans went to prison between 1933 and 1939 for expressing views that ran counter to those of the state. Their fate reflected the dark side of Hitler's hold on the German people. To be sure that hold

Socialist Erich Sander, arrested during the Nazi's first roundup of political opponents in 1933, took this picture of himself in his cell at Siegburg, a high-security prison near Cologne. Sander spent 10 years in prison and died just three months before his scheduled release.

never slackened, the Nazis developed one of the most effective—and fearsome—national police organizations the world has ever known. At its center were two men: Heinrich Himmler, leader of the Schutzstaffel, or SS, the armed guard of the Nazi Party; and his deputy Reinhard Heydrich, head of the Sicherheitsdienst, or SD, an intelligence service within the SS.

After a period of infighting typical of the Nazi leadership, Himmler had wrested de facto control of the Prussian police from Hermann Göring and had gained command of Germany's other regional police forces as well. Himmler merged them into one body and gave it a name that would become synonymous with unrestrained terror: Gestapo, short for Geheime Staatspolizei, the State Secret Police. In 1936, Hitler recognized Himmler's predominant position by officially naming him chief of police for all of Germany. Himmler used the appointment to merge the SD—which Reinhard Heydrich had built into a vast network of spies and informers—and the Gestapo, which used the information gathered by the SD to crush every semblance of opposition to Nazi rule.

Heading both the Gestapo and the SD was Heydrich, whose avowed ambition was to endow his command with a reputation for "brutality, inhumanity bordering on the sadistic, and ruthlessness." A colleague, mixing metaphors, called Heydrich "a living card index, a brain that held all the threads and wove them together." Even Hitler called him "the man with an iron heart."

Heydrich's network of agents, checking, prying and reporting to him in confidence from all over Germany, ranged in status from high-ranking party officials to volunteer *Hilfshauswarten* (roughly, "deputy house wardens"), who were in charge of sections of apartment buildings. By 1939 the SD boasted 570,000 unpaid local cell and block leaders, who were aided in turn by an estimated additional 1.5 million "assistants." This meant one Nazi was monitoring the lives of every 40 citizens throughout the Reich, from the great cities of the north to the isolated farming communities of the south.

Ostensibly, Heydrich's community force existed to carry out modest administrative duties on behalf of the government—collecting for the "Winter Help," the annual Christmas charity drive, and making sure that swastika flags flew on important days. But its members also carefully reported anything that appeared to be suspicious or critical of the party. The *Hoheitstraeger*, a publication for Nazi Party officials, asserted in 1938 that every local official "must be able to spot an un-German political attitude—liberal, Jewish, Marxist, etc." But speaking out of the other side of its mouth, the same publication cautioned in another issue: "The people must see in the local official a friend and helper, whom they can turn to for aid and advice. It would be awful and undesirable if the people regarded the official as a representative of the police."

Kennzeichen für Schutzhäftlinge in den Konz. Lagern

Form und Farbe der Kennzeichen

	Politisch	Berufs-Verbrecher	Emigrant	Bibel-forscher	Homo-sexuell	Asozial
Grund-farben	▼	▼	▼	▼	▼	▼
Abzeichen für Rückfällige	▼	▼	▼	▼	▼	▼
Häftlinge der Straf-kompanie	▼●	▼●	▼●	▼●	▼●	▼●
Abzeichen für Juden	✡	✡	✡	✡	✡	✡
Besondere Abzeichen	✡ Jüd. Rasse-schänder	▲ Rasse-schänderin	◉ Flucht-verdächtig	2307 Häftlings-Nummer		Beispiel
	P Pole	T Tscheche	▲ Wehrmacht Angehöriger	⬤ Häftling Ia		

A chart from Dachau depicts the complex system of patches used to identify inmates of concentration camps. In the top row, colored triangles designate general categories: red for political prisoners; green, criminals; brown, attempted emigrants; purple, religious fundamentalists; pink, homosexuals; black, "asocial" types. The second through fourth rows show more specific classifications: a stripe for repeat offenders; black disk, special punishment companies; superimposed yellow triangle, Jews. In the bottom two rows, categories are even more specific: black triangles for male and female "race defilers"; red disk, escape risks; serial number (issued to each prisoner); letters, foreigners; red triangle, members of the armed forces; arm band, the feeble-minded. The illustration at lower right shows a typical patch arrangement worn on the right leg of a prisoner's uniform.

Many of these minor Nazis in fact appeared to be harmless, and probably were. Christabel Bielenberg, an Englishwoman who, as the wife of a Hamburg lawyer, witnessed life in Nazi Germany before and during the War, remembered at least one block warden as an easygoing fellow. He was a gardener named Neisse. "On weekdays," Frau Bielenberg recalled, "Herr Neisse was friendly, gentle, even a little diffident; a well-shaped tree, the little dark corner where the lily of the valley needed some coaxing—those were matters for his obvious concern. On Sundays, things looked different. Resplendent then in brown uniform with shining boots and pillbox hat, his mustache trimmed to a neat rectangle, his left thumb hitched in his belt and his right arm raised rigid in salute, he was resurgent Germany." The Nazi gardener, of course, had nothing but praise for Adolf Hitler. "The Führer loves children," Neisse would tell Christabel Bielenberg, "and dogs, he loves dogs too."

Not all neighborhoods had such mild wardens, as another Hamburg resident, Olga Krueger, found out. Frau Krueger, a 38-year-old mother of six, had a brother and a brother-in-law who had been sent to concentration camps for displeasing the Nazis. One day, while having a sociable cup of coffee with her next-door neighbor, Frau Krueger made the mistake of letting slip her annoyance with the regime. Noticing a picture of Hitler on the wall, she exclaimed, "Oh, turn that face around. I cannot stand seeing him any longer."

The neighbor, who was also the neighborhood Nazi warden, said nothing. But the next day Olga Krueger received a summons to report to local party headquarters to explain her remark. Her husband, maintaining a cool head, pointed out that it was his wife's word against her neighbor's; as there had been no other witnesses, she could deny that she had ever made the statement about Hitler. Frau Krueger was an honest woman and she found it difficult to lie. But she managed to do so, and as a result she escaped punishment, after being upbraided for having greeted her inquisitors with a conventional "Good morning" instead of "Heil Hitler."

As instances of close calls like Frau Krueger's mounted, Germans learned to hold their tongues in the presence of both strangers and friends. Not even family members were safe from one another's informing. In the little Moselle

Adolf Hitler and Nazi notables tour the Great German Art Exhibition, passing an example of sculpture the Führer called "inspiringly beautiful human types."

A SHOW OF SCORN FOR UNSANCTIONED ART

The Nazis gave German artists four years to conform to official cultural policy—from the party's ascendancy in 1933 to the gala opening of the first Great German Art Exhibition in Munich in July 1937. Attended by Hitler, Joseph Goebbels, Hermann Göring and other officials, the exhibition prescribed what the Nazis considered to be the proper subjects of art. These were: a return to a mythic Aryan golden age, national and ethnic unity, pastoral scenes featuring robust peasants, and perfectly proportioned herculean bodies.

The day after the opening, the Nazis unveiled a separate exhibition that they titled "Degenerate Art." Intended to suggest the cultural corruption of the pre-Nazi regime, it was an eclectic display of outlawed modernist paintings and statuary by 112 artists. The works were given derogatory labels such as, "Thus did sick minds view nature." A cryptic message on the wall admonished: "They had four years' time."

Art was rated degenerate if it had a Jewish theme or was created by a Jewish artist such as Marc Chagall, if it was done by antiwar protestors such as Otto Dix and George Grosz, or if, in the opinion of arbiters at the Chamber of Culture, the subjects were ugly or deformed—signs of genetic or racial weakness.

Perhaps the most scathing commentary on the painters Hitler called "saboteurs of art" was a display labeled "Consummate Madness," in which the abstract works of Paul Klee, Jean Metzinger and others were unfavorably compared with works by inmates of mental asylums.

Both exhibitions to an extent fulfilled the Nazis' expectations. Said one visitor after viewing the "degenerate" art: "The artists ought to be tied up next to their pictures, so that every German can spit in their faces." Nevertheless, the prospect of sampling forbidden art proved irresistible: Two million people came to see the "degenerates," at least three times as many as attended the exhibition of sanctioned art.

The Rabbi by Marc Chagall was labeled "artistic bolshevism."

The Nazis outlawed Otto Dix's War Cripples, calling it "military sabotage."

Paul Klee's painting Villa R was called a worthless "concoction."

Wilhelm Lehmbruck's Kneeling Woman was deemed not "German" enough.

township of Wittlich, 21-year-old Franz Schroeder, who was the son of the neighborhood warden, was taken into "protective custody" by the authorities for being "a radio criminal." It seemed he was in the habit of listening to radio broadcasts from Luxembourg—only 50 miles away. Some time thereafter, his mother received an urn containing the ashes of her son, and a note saying that while in custody Franz had died of pneumonia—an improbable story, as the young man had been in perfect health when he was arrested. She concluded that the elder Schroeder had turned in his own son, and she never spoke to her husband again as long as he lived.

After 1936, fewer and fewer arrested persons were released, and those who did return to their homes and families were forbidden to talk about their experiences, under penalty of death. In reality, of course, they did talk—and in fact, such discussion served the Nazis' goal, which was to eliminate opposition by filling the citizens with fear.

One young worker, Haennes Maydag, who was arrested for being a Socialist, had what came to be recognized as a typical experience. "They came for me at five in the morning," he later recalled, "two big bulls in leather coats. They caught me in bed. I tried to get out by the back door, but one of them was waiting for me there. 'Gestapo,' he said, and showed me his badge.

"A minute later they had the cuffs on me and we were off in a motorcycle sidecar to Hamburg. There they gave me the usual 'first rubdown'—half a dozen of them banging me back and forth from one side of the room to the other. I lost half a dozen teeth that day. Later they had me and another 'political' prisoner crouch under the table while they played cards, and when they wanted to urinate they did it on me. I thought I could not take that kind of treatment. But I was in for a surprise. I was going to take a lot more—and worse—from the Gestapo before I saw the back of them."

Maydag spent the next 10 years in "protective custody" in a concentration camp—and lived to tell of it. Many people did not. By April 1939, German camps and prisons held 167,000 political prisoners. As war became imminent, thousands of them were condemned to death because, said a Justice Ministry official, "congenital criminal inclinations are easily aroused in wartime and the release of prisoners constitutes a danger to the community."

Whether or not they were singled out for arrest, as Haennes Maydag was, all German citizens had files with Heydrich's SD—and were classified according to how they should be dealt with in the event of mobilization. That monumental card index was one of Heydrich's more imagi-

Available in toy stores throughout Germany, this stuffed replica of an SA Brownshirt was one of several articles approved for sale by the government. Among the other items were an SS doll, a swastika Christmas-tree ornament and a picture of Hitler that lighted up.

native contributions; it enabled him to tell at a glance, by the color of a tab affixed to the top of each card, the political leanings of any citizen in the land. Those who fell into Heydrich's Group A-1—persons of such doubtful allegiance that they were to be arrested at once should the Führer decide to mobilize the armed forces—were recorded on cards flagged with red tabs. Those in Group A-2—persons to be arrested when news of mobilization was made public—were designated in blue. Those in Group A-3—people whose "apprehension or close supervision must be considered"—were designated with green tabs. Other colors indicated further refinements: Communist Party members rated dark red tabs and "Marxists" light red; mere grumblers were indicated in violet.

The German people may not have been aware of Heydrich's color-coded files. But by 1939 they were so wary of being denounced that they had developed the habit of looking over first one shoulder, then the other, before voicing a thought aloud. They gave the nervous trait a name: "the German look."

The fact that Germans could joke about their furtiveness did not reflect any reluctance to stand behind their Führer; some complaining was expected. "These days if you don't grumble about the government you stand out in the pubs," one German wrote to a friend abroad. Another remarked, "We Germans have always been good at grumbling, haven't we!" Germans felt that Hitler had fulfilled his promises—and had made Germany the better for it. He had provided jobs, built roads, increased food production, created an impressive Army, Navy and Air Force, and turned out a healthy, happy generation of young people.

What was more, Hitler had nullified the hated Versailles Treaty, reclaiming and indeed expanding German territory—and in doing so he had outmaneuvered Germany's World War I conquerors, Great Britain and France. In 1936 he had restored German troops to the Rhineland, the Versailles-dictated buffer zone along the French border. In the spring of 1938 his annexation of Austria added 6.5 million German-speaking citizens to the Reich, and in March of 1939 he had established a "protectorate" in part of Czechoslovakia, bringing in almost 10 million more citizens and a rich armaments industry as well. In all three instances the British and French had tried to halt Hitler through diplomacy—only to back down when he moved in troops to back his claims.

So far, Hitler's bold moves had cost not a drop of German blood. Clearly, the other powers were listening when the Führer spoke, and they seemed to be intimidated by the military force he had built up. Thus when Hitler announced that Germany must reclaim the Free City of Danzig, and with it the Polish Corridor, which separated East Prussia from the rest of the Reich, most Germans assumed that Britain and France would give in, as they had before.

The Allied powers, however, had grown tired of acquiescing. They were beginning to see that Hitler must be stopped before he threatened their own borders. In August of 1939, the British government signed a pact with Poland, promising to come to the Poles' assistance should Germany attack; France and Poland had long had a similar agreement. Both Britain and France continued to negotiate with Hitler, but with dwindling patience.

For the German people, the summer of 1939 was a time of almost palpable tension—especially in Berlin. Everywhere around them the people could see ominous signs that a storm was about to break. The squares and parks and other open places sprouted antiaircraft guns, their long barrels angled menacingly toward the empty sky. British and French nationals were packing their bags and leaving the country. Embassies were preparing to close. On August 27 came the surest indication yet that trouble lay ahead: The government announced that food rationing would commence the following day. And on the 28th the people of Berlin woke to see gray-clad troops surging through the city in every imaginable kind of vehicle—all headed eastward in the direction of Poland.

On September 1, German tanks rolled across the border as part of a coordinated land, sea and air attack. Danzig fell, but the Poles fought back, and they called on Britain and France to stand by their treaty obligations. The time of bloodless expansion had run out; Adolf Hitler had led the German *Volk* into war.

GIRDING FOR AN AIR WAR

Masked against anticipated poison-gas bombs, students and teachers in Potsdam assemble for the first day of the school year in late August of 1939.

"TODAY LEAFLETS, TOMORROW THE BOMBS"

Air Minister Hermann Göring was determined to make Germans the most air-power-conscious people on earth. To this end he perpetrated a gigantic propaganda stunt on the citizens of Berlin. Morning newspapers on June 24, 1933, carried accounts of mysterious foreign aircraft that had "bombed" the capital with anti-German leaflets. And embedded in the city's blooming parks were found ugly black-finned bomb casings. The news stories had been planted by an Air Ministry official, the dummy bombs by members of a new organization called the *Reichsluftschutzbund* (RLB), or Air Protection League.

The stunt had a dual purpose: to emphasize a disarmed Germany's vulnerability to aerial attack and to rally volunteers and donations for a civil-defense program. "Today it is only our enemy's leaflets, tomorrow it will be bombs," the government-inspired headlines warned. "Germans, arm yourselves, form air-protection groups." Posters aimed at the young mixed the threat of annihilation from the air with the promise of security through preparedness: "Save your pfennigs for the RLB," they urged, "and live to grow up."

These scare tactics, reinforced by realistic air-raid drills, sent Germans flocking to join the Air Protection League and enroll in courses in fire fighting and bomb-shelter construction. Over the next six years, Germany developed a civil-defense service of several thousand professionals and 13 million volunteers. Together they staged an annual "civil defense awareness week" to demonstrate survival techniques and equipment in city plazas and department stores.

Throughout the year, league members helped the police and fire departments direct air-raid drills. Block wardens taught householders to screen their windows to keep light in and bomb shards out. The government issued a "people's mask" to protect civilians against poison-gas bombs. Children practiced wearing the uncomfortable masks at school assemblies, and mothers learned to pressurize bellows-inflated gas capes for their infants and toddlers. As a result of such preparations, Germans in 1939 were as ready as any people could be to face the terrors of war from the air.

Berliners enter a theatrically marked public air-raid shelter during one of the many prewar civil-defense exercises held in the German capital.

Learning by doing, Berlin residents erect a lightproof blackout screen at an air-defense school in 1939. Any citizen could be jailed for blackout violations.

Garbed and masked against fire and gas, a civil-defense team prepares to douse an imaginary bomb with sand. Germany had initiated large-scale gas warfare

Mothers demonstrate two kinds of gas capes designed for infants and small children.

Mannequins model protective equipment in a window display labeled "gas defense."

in World War I and prudently prepared for retaliation in 1939.

Residents practice forming a bucket brigade to put out a rooftop fire.

Air-raid wardens of both sexes line up for inspection before a training session in damage control. The volunteer wardens were empowered to direct other citizens in fighting fires and clearing bomb wreckage.

Shreds of flaming phosphorus erupt as an airman pumps water toward the center of an incendiary bomb. The Germans learned the best way to deal with an incendiary: Smother it with sand or an umbrella of water.

A workman paints a white circle on a wooden traffic island in Berlin. White markings on curbs and other obstacles helped citizens avoid them during blackouts.

DISGUISING BERLIN TO DECOY THE ENEMY

Proud of the air defenses he had built since 1933, Hermann Göring often boasted that no enemy bomber ever would strike the city of Berlin. One stratagem by which he hoped to make good his vow was to disguise the city's landmarks as forests, black out almost all its lights, and decoy night-flying British bombers into hitting faintly illuminated dummy structures erected several miles away.

Just in case, however, the city fathers began to sheathe Berlin's museums, murals and monuments with bricks and sandbags. Portable treasures—eventually including paintings looted from conquered France and Holland—were packed away in crates to be stored in vaults underground. As they watched workmen shroud the broad boulevards in camouflage netting and paint blackout markers on the curbs, few Berliners could avoid pangs of foreboding.

Pedestrians stroll beneath camouflage netting supported by poles on the Charlottenburger Chaussee near

Berlin's Brandenburg Gate in late 1939. Strips of brown and green burlap laced in the netting simulated the evergreen groves that flanked the boulevard.

Workers shield a frieze depicting a battle from Greek mythology in Berlin's Pergamon Museum. Such precautions saved a number of cultural treasures from blast damage.

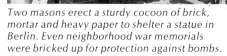

Two masons erect a sturdy cocoon of brick, mortar and heavy paper to shelter a statue in Berlin. Even neighborhood war memorials were bricked up for protection against bombs.

Dutch painter Rembrandt van Rijn's "Man in a Golden Helmet," a war trophy from the Netherlands, is crated for underground storage in Berlin's Karl-Friedrich Museum in 1941.

A museum window receives a sandbag screen in September 1939. The weather-resistant jute bags were scarce, and only museums got them.

Artificial smoke, simulating bomb-ignited fires, pours from buildings in the Wilhelmstrasse, Berlin's government center, as Luftwaffe bombers pass overhead during a midday air-raid drill.

REHEARSALS HEAVY WITH REALISM

Drill, drill, drill was Nazi Germany's solution to minimizing the effect of enemy bombs that—whatever Hermann Göring had promised—might soon fall on German cities. Once the War began, the pace of preparation grew more urgent; civilians practiced fire fighting and first aid while German bombers droned overhead and smoke bombs erupted in their wake.

Civil-defense officials were correct in anticipating that Royal Air Force bombers would someday break through the air-defense screen to scatter high-explosive and incendiary bombs on the homeland. But they expected that municipal fire fighters backed by well-drilled civilian volunteers would be able to limit the damage.

To make sure there were enough volunteers, a law passed in 1935 had decreed that "all Germans will be obliged to render such services as are necessary for the execution of air defense." By the time Allied bombing began in earnest in 1942, Germany's 80 million citizens had been thoroughly schooled in the protection of their lives and property.

Berlin fire fighters reel out hoses and raise ladders to the Reich Chancellery

Accompanied by a fire-policeman, bandaged citizens posing as casualties grope through smoke and over hoses after receiving first aid.

(left) and the Propaganda Ministry (rear). Regular firemen were instructed to concentrate on public buildings while volunteers dealt with residential fires.

2

A bland reaction to the outbreak of war
An anxious Hitler explains his invasion
Hurried evacuation from the western frontier
A ban on listening to foreign news
"Snake lines" at food stores
The nocturnal slaughter of a black-market pig
A church tower built with "coffee money"
Bringing home booty from conquered lands
A premature declaration of success
Marriage to a slain soldier
Hiding the casualties of the Eastern Front
A foretaste of airborne destruction

On the morning of September 1, 1939, the German people awoke to find their country at war. In Berlin, that momentous Friday broke gray and sultry with a hint of thunderstorms in the leaden clouds that hung overhead. The capital city seemed enveloped by an unnatural stillness. During the morning rush hour, streets that normally were noisy and bustling bore little traffic; the usual cacophony of auto horns had subsided to an occasional beep. Only the cries of the newsboys, hawking extra editions that carried the first stories of war, disturbed the abnormal silence. The headlines screamed, but the pedestrians who stopped to read them were grim-faced and subdued.

Berlin was a city in shock. "War broke quietly, as if under a cloud," wrote Werner Harz, a German journalist. "There were no frenzied people in the streets such as we read about in 1914. No flags, no processions. No cheering, no marching troops or flowers. The streets of Berlin seemed empty. There was only a particularly dull sense of waiting."

The apathy that pervaded the capital on that first morning of World War II was repeated in Germany's other great cities, and in its towns and villages. Yet apathy was not a universal response among the country's population of 80 million. Loyal Nazis embraced their Führer's action as the only means of achieving the complete resurrection of Germany. Swayed by propaganda, encouraged by Hitler's unblemished record of diplomatic coups, they greeted the War with enthusiasm and confidence: "No need to worry at all," a Berlin office manager told one of his employees that morning. "You can take my word for it—this war against Poland will be just a blitzkrieg. It will be over in a flash."

An even warmer response came from Germany's male youth, who had been meticulously conditioned for such an event. Just as the Nazi leadership had anticipated, the young men of Germany saw the War as a glorious adventure: Julius Hacketeil, a 17-year-old schoolboy, declared to his friends, "I shall volunteer for the Army tomorrow morning!" Harald Juhnke, a 10-year-old member of the *Jungvolk,* the junior branch of the Hitler Youth, desperately wanted to join the fight. "Why couldn't I become a soldier now?" he recalled wondering. "The Nazis had convinced us that the whole world threatened us, and I wanted to defend the fatherland."

But neither the ardor of the faithful nor the fervor of youth

DELUSIONS OF QUICK VICTORY

could dispel the gloom that settled on the mass of German people that day. It infected all ages, all classes and all walks of life. Admiral Wilhelm Canaris, the brilliant chief of the Abwehr, the Wehrmacht's intelligence and espionage agency, was one of those who had considered Hitler the savior of the country. But when Canaris was advised of the impending invasion of Poland, he turned to a colleague and whispered: "This means the end of Germany." Former heavyweight boxing champion Max Schmeling (who in 1938 had lost to Joe Louis in an attempt to regain his crown) had just returned home with his new wife, the Czech movie star Anny Ondra. "So, Anny," he said sadly to his bride after hearing of the invasion, "now there's going to be a catastrophe!"

Schmeling's dismay was shared by a high-school girl, Ilse Heimerdinger of Altenburg, who got the news on that fateful morning when her headmaster began writing on the blackboard. "I stepped nearer and my eyes fixed on the words, 'War has been declared,'" she recalled later. "The next thing I remembered was the anxious face of my classmate bending over me. I had blacked out. I should have been proud and happy like the Hitler Youth; instead I was deeply disappointed and terribly shocked that Hitler was not great enough to avert such a catastrophe."

There was sound reason behind the reluctance of most Germans to respond to their government's call to arms with cheers and flowers. Too well they remembered World War I. Scarcely an adult in Germany had not experienced the deprivations and horrors of that war, either firsthand or through the travails of relatives. It had begun in great celebration, but its bleak legacy was evidence that another conflict on such a scale would end not in honor and glory for Germany, but in renewed sorrow and suffering.

For all their dread of what lay ahead, Germans were powerless to alter the chain of events set in motion by their leader that day. Though the government had failed in its efforts to generate widespread enthusiasm for the War, it retained its iron grip on the will of the people. With few exceptions, the Germans had lost their voices. No longer did they have a say in shaping their own destiny; mutely they followed their Führer into the War. For the next six years, their fortunes would follow the tumultuous course laid out by Adolf Hitler. At times that course would seem to lead them tanta-

lizingly close to peace, but then it would wrench them back to the brink of despair. And the path would end where many already feared it would—in an inferno of terror and death.

While Germans tried to assimilate the news that their country was once more at war, the man responsible attempted to explain his actions to his people, and to the world. At 10 a.m. on September 1, Hitler addressed the Reichstag. He cited Polish aggression as the cause of the conflict, in particular accusing the Poles of attacking a radio station in the German town of Gleiwitz, near the border between the two countries. The Führer neglected to mention, of course, that the attack was a sham—carried out by Germans disguised in Polish uniforms to provide an excuse for the invasion.

As Hitler spoke, there were indications that he shared his people's misgivings about the new conflict. His mood was serious and seemed tinged with anxiety. Even a hint of discouragement entered Hitler's voice, noted American correspondent William L. Shirer. "Though truculent at times," Shirer wrote, "he seemed strangely on the defensive, and throughout the speech ran a curious strain, as though he himself were dazed at the fix he had got himself into and felt a little desperate about it. Somehow he did not carry conviction, and there was much less cheering in the Reichstag than on previous, less important occasions."

Hitler had reason to be subdued, for a crucial question loomed over the Reichstag that morning: Would Poland's allies, France and England, honor their treaty obligations and come to her aid? Or was Foreign Minister Joachim von Ribbentrop correct in his assessment that these two strong nations were in no mood to commit themselves to war? Hitler had gambled that Ribbentrop was right, but he was covering his bet: Preparations to meet an attack from the West had already begun, and with them came the first of the hardships that the German people would have to endure.

The evacuation of civilians from Germany's western frontier—the so-called Red Zone along the borders of Belgium, Luxembourg and France—began in the middle of the night on September 1. Between the cities of Aachen to the north and Saarbrücken to the south, village after village was rudely awakened. The startled inhabitants of Prüm, in the Eifel region on the Belgian border, were roused from their beds at about 3 a.m. by the village crier, an institution in many small German towns. He stumbled through the dark, cobbled streets ringing his bell and shouting that everyone must leave immediately, taking no more than 33 pounds of luggage. By dawn the villagers were packed in trucks and on their way to the safer interior. Only 12 civilians, selected to look after the village's precious livestock, remained. Although it was the middle of the harvest season, no one was left to gather the crops now ripening in the fields; that night the village of Prüm was ruined financially.

Elsewhere in the rugged Eifel it was the same. At the village of Berscheid, the mayor woke the citizens at 4 a.m. and demanded that they be ready to evacuate within four hours. "All our protesting and pleading didn't help," the village chronicler recorded. "We had to go, our hearts heavy with the unspoken question: Would we ever see one another again in this life?"

Many of them would not. The people of Berscheid and other villages were trucked to larger townships in the border area, where special trains were waiting to carry them, by the thousands, deeper into the Reich. Young Katharina Hermes of Berscheid was taken with her fellow evacuees to the railroad station at the town of Neuerburg. As she waited for a train she watched the sad arrival of other unfortunate villagers. "Truckload after truckload, they kept rolling up," she wrote later. "Old men, women and children, sick and weak, young mothers with their babies at the breast, holding other children by the hand, school children with their school satchels on their backs, and all laden down with luggage, rucksacks, blankets and feather beds. They cried, they cursed, they shouted, they appealed to God and moaned and moaned. But there was no way out."

At daybreak the first of the packed trains began to move eastward. Early in the journey the evacuees met troop transports rolling slowly in the opposite direction, filled with soldiers heading for what would once more become the Western Front. Unlike the evacuees, Katharina Hermes recalled, the young men seemed to be in a buoyant mood: "They went to meet the enemy with the song, 'There'll Be a Reunion in the Homeland,' on their lips. Then there were other trains laden with tanks and artillery. Hundreds of trucks carrying ammunition filled the roads on both sides, too. Then regiment after regiment of infantry marching westward. It was a moving sight. All these young men in the prime of life moving toward their deaths, sooner or later."

Elsewhere in Germany, newly printed posters tacked up in the streets informed the people of wartime rules and regulations that would govern their lives. Blackouts went into immediate effect, and with them true night descended on Germany. As the sun went down on the cities, darkness crept into the streets. With the darkness came a peculiar silence, as though the ban on light were also a ban on sound. Virtually all traffic disappeared except for the trolleys, buses and elevated trains, which made their rounds with pale blue bulbs casting an unearthly luminescence throughout their interiors. Passengers' faces took on the pallor of the dead; conversations were conducted in whispers.

Another new stricture—gasoline rationing—made personal automobiles a luxury of the past. Only vehicles used "in the national interest" were allowed fuel. All over Germany, autos went into storage for the duration. As the volume of motor traffic in the cities fell dramatically, bicycles were cleaned and oiled and put back on the road.

Food rationing commenced almost as the first guns were fired. Each German family was instructed to report to its local food office to pick up color-coded ration cards: blue for meat, yellow for dairy products, white for sugar, green for

eggs, orange for bread, pink for cereals and purple for fruits. Meat was limited to 15½ ounces per person a week, and two meatless days each week were decreed for restaurants.

Though the rationing of food spurred a wave of complaint, its impact at first was superficial. Germans had grown used to living on restricted amounts of food, a result of the government's stockpiling in preparation for war. The people already had experienced shortages of coffee, dairy products and fruit. By and large they had remained healthy, and the new rationing would not force them to tighten their belts much. Only later, as events on the battlefield forced changes at home, did the question of food become serious.

Far more ominous in the first days of the conflict were the grim warnings on street posters concerning crimes against the state. Listening to foreign radio stations was punishable by a minimum of five years in prison—or by death. With the edict, the German government tried to sever the last ties between its people and the outside world. From now on, they would hear only what the Führer wished them to.

Sunday, September 3, dawned a beautiful late-summer day in Berlin. As though peace still prevailed, Berliners flocked to the woods and lakes of their suburbs. It seemed that the War might be only a bad dream—that no German planes were bombing Polish cities, that no German tanks were sweeping across the Polish plain.

In the ornate Reich Chancellery, however, the War was an ominous reality. At 9 a.m. Sir Nevile Henderson, the British Ambassador, handed a note to Dr. Paul Schmidt, Ribbentrop's interpreter. It was an ultimatum from the British government: Unless Germany agreed by 11 a.m. to withdraw its troops from Poland, a state of war would exist between Great Britain and Germany. Schmidt accepted the note and hurried to the Chancellery. After jostling his way through the crowd of Cabinet members and others in Hitler's anteroom, he entered the Führer's office. Hitler was sitting at his desk; Ribbentrop was standing by a window.

"Both looked up tensely when they caught sight of me," Schmidt wrote later. "I stopped some distance from Hitler's desk and slowly translated the British government's ultimatum. When I finished there was dead silence.

"Hitler sat immobile, staring into space. He sat absolutely silent and unmoving. After an interval, which seemed an eternity to me, he turned to Ribbentrop, who had remained standing frozen by the window. 'What now?' Hitler asked his Foreign Minister with a furious glare, as if to say that Ribbentrop had misinformed him about the probable reaction of the British. Ribbentrop replied in a muted voice: 'I assume that within the hour the French will hand us a similar ultimatum.' "

By noon, newsboys were selling a new extra: England had declared war; France soon followed. In Berlin's Wilhelmplatz, a public square near the Chancellery, a crowd of some 250 people heard the ever-present loudspeakers squawking for attention. Observing the crowd was William Shirer. "They listened attentively to the announcement," Shirer wrote in his diary. "When it was finished, there was not a murmur. They just stood there as they were before. Stunned. The people cannot realize yet that Hitler has led them into a world war."

In the weeks that followed, German civilians saw little evidence that their country actually was engaged in a great

"Hamster! Shame on you!" declares a poster that uses a pun on the similar German words for hamster and hoarding—"Hamsterin" and "Hamstern"—to make its point. To combat hoarding, German police raided cellars to confiscate caches of food. Eventually even the booty sent home by soldiers was counted against their families' ration cards.

A grocer scoops sauerkraut into a dish brought from home by a customer. By 1940, a scarcity of paper for bags and packages forced shoppers to carry their own containers.

war. There were no attacks on their western frontier, no air raids on their cities. All the news they received was welcome: German armies were advancing in rapid thrusts through Poland, the Polish Air Force had been crushed, Warsaw had fallen. Gradually, the tension that had gripped Germany melted, and life settled into a new routine.

Much of the routine centered on food. There was enough to keep a person healthy—bread and potatoes were plentiful—but shortages of some items made for an intolerably monotonous diet. Fish and chicken were available only at certain times. Fruit remained a rarity, and coffee was worth nearly its weight in gold. The quest for a varied diet began to possess the German housewife, and gave birth to the phenomenon called *Schlangestehen,* or "standing in snakes," as the food lines were popularly known.

"On market days I had to be out as early as possible," recalled Christabel Bielenberg, the Englishwoman who was married to a German and had recently arrived in Berlin. "If one didn't know a store owner, cows suddenly had no liver, no heart and no kidneys, and chickens had disappeared from the face of the earth. Suddenly, hoarding became a time-consuming occupation—for some people their main activity. Posters such as 'The good of the community goes before that of the individual' and 'German woman, your Führer relies on you' could be seen on every second billboard in Berlin, but they made absolutely no impression on the brave housewives out scrummaging for food."

Housewives generally had first crack at the available food. Office workers could only join long lines in their off-hours and pray that something would be left when their turn came. Too often they were bitterly disappointed; tempers grew short, spurring arguments, name-calling and sometimes even small-scale riots.

When the problem of the queues loomed large enough to attract the attention of corpulent Reich Marshal Hermann Göring, he publicly expressed a fatherly concern. Word of Göring's solicitude was received in the food lines with bitter laughter. "Old fatso should come here and stand for a few days," said a woman waiting at a fish market. "That would help his weight problem."

The shortages of coveted foodstuffs inevitably gave rise to a thriving black market, an institution familiar to Germans who recalled the days of World War I. The black market in food was at its most active close to the source of supply, the farms. People from the cities began to spend their free days on cross-country jaunts trying to barter or buy food from local farmers. Rural policemen took to stopping city folk carrying suspicious-looking bags to search them for black-market goods. Soon the newspapers, on Goebbels' orders, began printing the details of severe sentences passed on black marketeers, such as long internment in concentration camps and sometimes even death. Neither the penalties nor Goebbels' scare tactics had much effect.

In time, the black market became the last resort for tens of thousands of frustrated Germans. One of them was 25-year-old Hilde Leitz, who lived in the town of Wittlich. Although she worked in the County Food Office and helped herself liberally to ration coupons, Fräulein Leitz could not obtain enough meat for herself and her aging parents. So in the late fall of 1939 she decided, in her word, to "organize" a pig. One night a willing farmer outside town sold her a pig on the black market. She and her mother put the animal in a baby carriage, gave it a pint of schnapps to drink in order to keep it quiet, and wheeled it back home to Wittlich under the noses of the local police.

Now the two women faced the problem of slaughtering

A German passenger car tows a hefty trailer in a demonstration of home-front innovations to cope with shortages of heavy transport and fuel. The automobile's rear wheels have been connected to an auxiliary axle to provide extra drive, and its engine has been converted to run on synthetic fuel, stored in canisters mounted on the trunk.

the pig—a task they had never attempted—without having its squeals disturb neighbors, who might well denounce them. They also feared waking Fräulein Leitz's father, who was snoring upstairs; he was the Nazi neighborhood leader and, as his daughter recalled, he would have "thrown a fit if he had found out what we were doing." After much hesitation the two women managed to slit the hog's throat while smothering its cries, and they spent the rest of the night transforming its carcass into sausages and chops. At dawn they fell into bed exhausted, with all traces of the illegal operation scrubbed away and the meat safely hidden.

On the edges of the flourishing domestic black market, the smuggling of foodstuffs into the Reich from neighboring countries developed on a large scale, and for good reason: By 1941 a pound of coffee smuggled from Holland or Belgium brought $20 in Berlin. With wartime inflation, coffee became more valued than the reichsmark; the Germans called it coffee currency, and it became the most desired form of payment.

Smugglers risked their lives to run the contraband. In the Ardennes-Eifel region on the Belgian border, they faced not only rugged terrain but the German West Wall, a forbidden military zone where trespassing could carry the death penalty. Yet smuggling became a major local industry: The tower of one of the churches was named "Saint Coffee's Steeple" because it was paid for by donations from parishioners who had earned the money smuggling coffee beans.

As the autumn of 1939 stiffened into winter, the weather grew exceptionally severe and the Nazi regime faced its first major test at home—a coal crisis. Although coal supplies adequate to keep Germany warm were stockpiled at the mines, not enough trains were available to transport the coal to the cities. In the great industrial push to prepare the armed forces for war, the regime had neglected to build enough new freight cars and locomotives, and the conquest and occupation of Poland had claimed many of the existing trains. As the temperature plummeted, canals and rivers froze solid, paralyzing the barge traffic that might otherwise have alleviated the shortage of rail transport.

At the mines, the coal piled up; in the industrial centers, work slowed down and in some cases stopped altogether, leaving thousands of men temporarily out of work. Germans shivered in their frigid homes, and in the absence of an explanation from their government, they complained bitterly.

Nothing seemed to be happening in the War that winter to justify the nagging privations the Germans were enduring: the blackouts, the food rationing and the shortages. The armies of Western Europe were quiet. England and France seemed content to remain on the defensive, behind their frontiers. At some points German sentries pacing along the West Wall could see their French counterparts patrolling the nearby Maginot Line. Sometimes enemy sentries would stop, wave at each other and trade insults. Loudspeakers on both sides began hurling barrages of propaganda across the lines, without visible effect on either side.

In their discontent, the German people came up with a label for their Führer's conflict: the *Sitzkrieg*, or "sit-down war." During this time of stagnation at the front, rumors ran wild at home. Throughout the winter the most persistent story held that a German offensive in the West was imminent—a thrust through neutral Belgium, and the Netherlands, and perhaps even little Luxembourg.

In the spring of 1940 the rumor became reality. Indeed, it had been understated. Hitler unleashed his armies, and one by one countries in Scandinavia and Western Europe tum-

Women typists keep warm in overcoats during the winter of 1939-1940. The military's need for coal left scant supplies for offices and still less for homes, even in such coal-rich regions as the Ruhr valley.

bled before the onslaught. Denmark and Norway were overrun, to be followed by Luxembourg, Holland and Belgium. By the end of June, France had fallen and only England remained to oppose the victorious Wehrmacht.

At home, the German people basked in the glow of these victories. The armistice with France erased the shame of their country's defeat in 1918; with their most powerful continental enemy out of the War, the way seemed clear for a quick settlement with England and an end to the conflict. Suddenly it seemed that the government's program of conquest had been right and logical all along. Nazi flags began flying from German homes where none had flown before. The new mood among the people was observed by the American, William Shirer: "Quite a few Germans are beginning to feel that the deprivations Hitler had forced on them have not been without reason. Said my room waiter this morning: 'Perhaps the English and French now wish they had less butter and more cannon.'"

In Berlin, a tangible sign of a quick end to the War came in the form of a German infantry division, recently returned from France, that paraded victoriously through the capital. Thousands of civilians turned out to cheer the soldiers. Reporting the scene was Howard K. Smith, an American radio newsman. "I saw real, uninhibited enthusiasm, with the

Germans weeping and laughing from pure, spontaneous joy," Smith wrote later. "The soldiers marched in clouds of confetti. Children broke through the police cordon and carried little bouquets of flowers to the marching soldiers, while a dozen military bands in the march played martial music. It was truly a glorious day. And in every happy heart lived the belief that this was the end to war."

Adding to the celebratory air was a newfound wealth of material goods—the spoils of war. Using artificially inflated reichsmarks, German soldiers in occupied countries were buying up the luxuries of Europe; for anyone with a relative in the armed forces, good things were available in abundance. "A soldier coming home on leave was a fine sight to see," Smith wrote. "In addition to his kit, he carried baskets, cardboard boxes and cheap suitcases filled to overflowing with all kinds of goodies from the 'front.'

"Suddenly charwomen and housemaids whose legs had never been caressed by silk began wearing silk stockings. Little street-corner taverns began displaying rows of Armagnac, Martell and Courvoisier. The streets were filled with gleeful servant girls wrapped in luxurious silver-fox fur coats from Norway."

In those heady months of 1940, a maxim was coined: "Enjoy the war, peacetime will be awful." Later, the words would be used in bitterness, but for now the saying had some merit. The Depression era was fully over; there was employment for everyone in the booming war industries, and money was plentiful. Middle-class families continued to hire domestic servants, many of them dragooned from Poland and other occupied countries. Despite the two meatless days a week, restaurants were packed and nightclubs overflowed. In the big cities, only the propaganda posters indicated that Germany was a nation at war.

Then, in the midst of this peaceful prosperity, the unthinkable occurred. On the night of August 25, Royal Air Force planes made their way to Berlin and bombed the city. It happened several more times during the following nights. The damage was modest and the casualties relatively few. But the impact of the raids went far beyond the damage they caused: For the first time in history, bombs had fallen on the capital city. The realization sent a shock wave through Germans everywhere.

"Berliners are stunned," wrote William Shirer. "They did

Laden with booty, a soldier on leave receives a warm welcome home. A generous exchange rate let German troops carry off the finest goods in Europe—Norwegian furs, Belgian coffee, and so much French perfume that Berlin, one resident complained, "smelled like a hairdresser's."

Parading through the Brandenburg Gate in July of 1940, troops of the Wehrmacht receive a victor's welcome to Berlin—complete with flowers from a young enthusiast—after crushing France in a six-week blitz.

not think that it could ever happen. When this war began Göring assured them that it couldn't, and they believed him. Their disillusionment therefore is all the greater. You have to see their faces to measure it."

The RAF raids infuriated the Nazi hierarchy. Goebbels launched a propaganda attack through the media, decrying the brutality of the British in bombing helpless women and children. The headlines of Berlin's dailies railed against the RAF: "Cowardly British Attack!" shrilled one. "British Air Pirates over Berlin!" proclaimed another. But Goebbels' efforts could not erase one fact: The German homeland was vulnerable.

As the months wore on, events outside Germany gave further warning to those at home that they faced another winter of war. Despite the Luftwaffe's efforts to bomb Britain into submission, the island kingdom refused to capitulate. Though greatly outnumbered, the Royal Air Force scored heavily against the German bombers and postponed forever Hitler's scheme to invade across the Channel. The peace that had seemed so near began to slip away.

The German people spent the winter of 1940-1941 enduring a renewed coal crisis and other privations, among them growing shortages of clothes and shoes. These two commodities had been stockpiled in sufficient quantities to see the nation through a short war, and rationing of them began in the autumn of 1939 to stretch the supply. But the conflict was far from over, and the factories that had produced shoes and textiles were now engaged in meeting the demands of the Wehrmacht. As a consequence, the German people were becoming threadbare and poorly shod.

The useful life of clothing and linen during these times was shortened by the soap that the German housewife was compelled to use. Called "people's soap," it came in grainy, greenish cakes and smelled of cheap perfume. The soap was abrasive, it melted away quickly with use and it produced suds only under the most vigorous scrubbing. To assuage the housewives, Goebbels' newspaper *Der Angriff* published a long article offering tips on the use of the detested cleanser: Save your soap scraps, it said, and keep them in a bag for personal washing, or warm the scraps in a muslin bag on the stove and press them into a homemade cake. *Der Angriff* also advised keeping a basin of soapy water available for family use, and using soda or sand instead of soap to clean the kitchen—suggestions that kindled little enthusiasm in the hearts of German housewives, who were accustomed to higher standards of cleanliness.

Beset by such irritations, the Germans passed their second winter of the War. Many clung to the notion that Eng-

land would come to terms and life would return to normal. "All winter," remembered Johannes Nosbüsch, a college professor, "the motto was 'There is only one enemy left—England.' More and more, England was presented as the real cause of the continued war." On Christmas Eve, the bells rang on the radio and the choir sang "Stille Nacht," and everyone felt certain that next year Christmas would be celebrated in a world at peace. But such optimists had no inkling of what their Führer even then was planning.

Early on the 22nd of June, 1941, Adolf Hitler inaugurated his "crusade in the East," the long-planned invasion of the Soviet Union. In German cities an extra edition of the Führer's own newspaper, the *Völkischer Beobachter,* was on the streets early, proclaiming the momentous news: "War Front from North Cape to Black Sea—The Reckoning with the Moscow Traitors—Two-faced Jewish Bolshevist Rulers in the Kremlin Lengthen the War for the Benefit of England!"

The single-sheet extras were grabbed up as soon as they appeared. As they had in 1939, people stood where they were, staring at the page, dumfounded. At first, the new turn of events hit them like a bombshell. Unlike their country's invasion of Poland, this attack had not been preceded by a telltale propaganda campaign. There had been no diatribes in the press or on the radio. The Soviet Union, in fact, had been an ally—one whose shipments of raw materials and finished goods had been helping Germany subvert the British sea blockade.

Surprise soon gave way to a sense of the inevitable. Germans remembered the Führer's prewar fulminations against the Bolsheviks, and many of them—the pro-Nazis in particular—felt that they understood the reasons behind his latest action. On the morning of the invasion, Harry Flannery, an American journalist on his way to a recording studio to broadcast the news to the United States, sensed a current of excitement flowing through the gathered crowds: "For the first time since the War had begun," he wrote later, "there was a momentary enthusiasm among the German populace. The war against Russia was the first popular campaign that had been launched. None of the Germans had ever been able to understand why a treaty should have been

made with the Soviets, since they had been made the main object of denunciation since 1933. Now they had a sense of relief, a feeling of final understanding. 'Now,' they said, 'we are fighting our real enemy.' ''

That exuberance was destined to last for some time. For the first few weeks of Operation *Barbarossa,* as the Wehrmacht swept deep into the Soviet Union, the mood on the German home front was buoyant. Day after day, regular programing on the state radio was interrupted by special communiqués from the military high command. In restaurants and cafés and other public places, the radio would be turned up, as the law demanded, so that people on the sidewalks could hear. Waiters stopped serving and diners stopped eating and talking. Then a blast of trumpets and a roll of drums introduced an announcer who delivered the news of yet another triumph of German arms.

Once more the German people began to sense the nearness of victory, to be followed by peace. ''The mood of the population has changed dramatically,'' government pollsters wrote in a report that summer. ''Today nobody takes Russia seriously as a military opponent. People are so confident that they are talking about a period of six weeks before the War is over.''

Such hopes were reinforced by Hitler's own optimism. In an address on October 3, 1941, he proclaimed victory over the Soviet Union: ''I declare today, without any reservation, that the enemy in the East has been struck down and will never rise again!''

Germans at home were slow to realize how wrong the Führer had been. Not so at the front. The Soviet armies, which had been bowled over by the surprise attack in June,

recouped during the autumn and mounted a savage resistance. As the weather grew cold, the German attack bogged down. The effort to capture Leningrad subsided into siege and stalemate, and the drive to capture Moscow failed dismally. All along the front, German troops dug in to endure the dreaded Russian winter.

Back home, the human cost of the Russian campaign was gradually becoming apparent. Harry Flannery noted the sudden appearance of wounded men in Berlin. ''Before the Russian campaign,'' he wrote, ''I saw a wounded soldier in the streets only now and again. But after it began I saw them in every block along the principal streets—young men with their arms in slings, with an arm gone, walking with crutches and canes, or without one of their legs. Previously too there had been few women in mourning, but I began to see them everywhere.''

As one result of the proliferation of grieving women, the government issued new regulations allowing the bizarre practice of marrying the dead. The purpose of the new law was to benefit pregnant women whose men had been killed in action; the ''marriage'' would give the unborn child a family name and provide the mother with the pension awarded to war widows. One young woman who took advantage of the law was Ilse Heimerdinger of Altenburg, whose fiancé, John Pilger, a Luftwaffe pilot, had been shot down over Russia and killed. Though she was not pregnant, Fräulein Heimerdinger agreed to the marriage at the urging of her fiancé's parents, who wanted to preserve their only son's name.

The ceremony took place in the local registrar's office, which was incongruously decorated with vases of flowers.

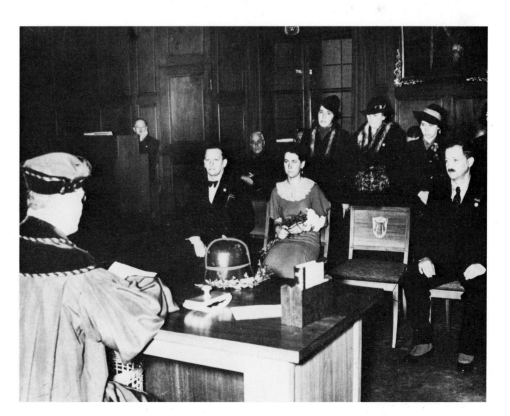

Curious neighbors watch as workmen repair modest bomb damage to a residential street in Berlin after an early Allied raid. Royal Air Force bombers hit the German capital for the first time on August 25, 1940—one day after the Luftwaffe first bombed London.

A helmet, a garland of flowers and an empty chair represent the absent bridegroom as a woman is married by proxy in a Munich courtroom. Special regulations allowed women to marry men who were away at the front and even fiancés who had died in combat.

Fräulein Heimerdinger sat next to a chair that bore the cap and sword of a Luftwaffe officer. After she said her vows to the dead man, the registrar declared her legally wed. As directed, the young woman signed her name in the marriage book; next to her signature she made a cross to represent her husband. Then the registrar shook her hand and presented her with a package, saying it was a gift from the German government.

"I walked out of the office in a daze," the new Frau Pilger recalled. "Once outside I unwrapped the parcel, and the brown packing paper revealed a black leather case with a book inside. I removed the book from the case and to my utter amazement found myself staring at the words, printed in gold: 'Adolf Hitler, *Mein Kampf.'*"

Realizing that the bleak situation on the battlefield could be disastrous to morale at home, the regime went to lengths to distort the truth. One scheme was devised to maintain the image of the Wehrmacht soldier as a victor returning with the spoils, as he had been during the conquest of Western Europe. After the first months of fighting, the scorched Russian earth no longer yielded booty, so Goebbels' propaganda experts came up with a substitute: a parcel containing, among other items, a sausage or two, a tin of meat and a bottle of schnapps. Labeled "Hitler's Gift," the package

was given to each soldier as he crossed the border of the Reich on leave.

As the Russian campaign grew worse, however, those soldiers most in need of rest were prohibited from visiting their relatives. They were sent instead to convalescent homes and recreation centers far from their families to prevent them from spreading the word about the situation in the Soviet Union. Other forms of censorship were put into effect as well. For the first time in the War, letters sent home from soldiers at the front were censored to eliminate any negative comments. On Goebbels' orders the daily newspapers, which had been full of death notices sent in by relatives of soldiers killed in action, restricted such announcements to only a handful per issue. And the wounded, thousands upon thousands of them, arrived in Germany secretly and received treatment at special hospitals, out of the public eye.

Inevitably, however, some Germans at home were to witness the carnage of the Russian campaign. One of them was Irma Krueger, a 15-year-old who was conscripted as an auxiliary nurse and assigned to tend the wounded at her school, which had been transformed into an emergency military hospital. "Normally we auxiliaries—all girls in our teens—would arrive at our old school about seven in the morning," Fräulein Krueger recalled. "The wounded would already be there, packed into the gymnasium by the hundreds. During the night they had been shunted off the main Berlin-Hamburg line onto the sidings at Reinbek, where the male orderlies were waiting with ambulances to collect them. Now they were stripped naked on the straw, covered with lice for the most part, with the orderlies moving along their ranks ripping off the plaster, and later in the War, the paper bandages that covered their wounds. We would help the best we could, forgetting that there were naked men on all sides. Then the sprinklers in the ceiling would be turned on, and if the wounded were lucky, lukewarm water would descend upon them, cleaning them up a little. If they were unlucky it would be cold, because there was a shortage of fuel. Then they would scream.

"Now the doctors passed among them," Irma Krueger continued, "selecting the ones they would operate upon first, not even bothering about those who had stomach wounds, because even if they did recover, they would no

Carrying a placard imploring people to give generously, used-clothing collectors of the Winter Relief Organization push their loaded cart down a Berlin street in 1942. Great pressure was sometimes put on those who refused to be generous. One widow asked to be taken into protective custody when an angry crowd smashed her greenhouse because she had offered only her riding boots to the clothing drive. In some towns, zealous collectors posted "Boards of Shame" to stigmatize the stingy.

Flag-waving children leave Berlin on an evacuation train. Some 500,000 youngsters were shipped off to safety in rural education camps, entire schools often moving as a unit. The schools were reestablished under Hitler Youth administrators, who took advantage of the absence of family and church influences to intensify Nazi indoctrination of the youngsters.

longer have any real fighting value. Thereafter the doctors would be operating all day long, their rubber boots and aprons a bright red with blood, and our old school janitor, Herr Schmitz, would be back and forth all the time, carrying sawed-off limbs under his arms to be burned in the school incinerators in the cellar. It was a terrible time.''

Not every civilian was subjected to such indelibly poignant scenes, but elsewhere there was ample if less dramatic evidence that the situation, both at home and at the front, was rapidly deteriorating. In German factories, substantial numbers of old men were called back to work as replacements for younger employees who had been drafted and sent to the East—to replace, in turn, men killed or wounded in action. And for the first time in the War, the government launched a major publicity campaign to recruit women for war industry (pages 72-87). All over the Reich, posters appeared displaying a female busy at a factory workbench. Upper-class women, in particular, were urged to seek employment for the first time in their lives. Teenagers too were now summoned to perform their duty: Boys of 16 and even younger appeared in uniform as "flak helpers," part-time antiaircraft crewmen.

The German High Command, having anticipated a swift victory, had neglected to issue winter gear to its troops fighting in the Soviet Union. In an emergency appeal, the government called upon the people to donate furs, woolens and boots—almost anything warm to wear—for the suffering soldiers. To many civilians, the regime's plea for help was a bald admission of failure—a revelation that discouraged many in the homeland.

Like their men at the front, German civilians were running short of warm clothes. Textile supplies, which had been scarce the year before, now dwindled to nothing: The Allied sea blockade prevented imports of raw materials, and such textile plants as existed could not meet the demands of the Wehrmacht, much less provide for civilians. As a consequence, clothing ration cards became worthless scraps of paper; many of them were offered, in dark humor, as contributions to the used-clothing drives organized by the government.

Bravely, some haberdasheries and dress shops in the cities still maintained lavish display windows, but these were merely façades; behind them the stores lay empty. Signs in the windows explained that the clothing on display could not be sold until the display had been changed—and, of course, it never was. Most shopkeepers had not even a stitch to put in their windows. One merchant in Berlin tried to make up the deficiency by filling his window with large boxes, each of which was empty. Then, in an honest but naïve gesture of loyalty, he hung a portrait of Hitler

above the display along with the legend, "We thank our Führer." Local Nazi Party officials were irate; one could not thank the Führer for empty boxes. They ordered the hapless shopkeeper to remove the display immediately.

The plight of the German merchant with nothing to sell gave rise to a bitter joke: After hearing that a court has sentenced a notorious murderer to be hanged, Hitler remarks to Göring that hanging is too quick for such a man,

that he should be starved to death slowly and painfully. "Quite right," Göring replies. "How about opening a small shop for him?"

Even worse than the clothing shortage as winter approached was Germany's first real food crisis since long before the War. Until now, the population had compensated for the scarcity of meat by eating vegetables—chiefly potatoes—which were plentiful and not rationed. Restaurants,

Its cathedral engulfed in smoke, the historic Baltic port of Lübeck burns after an RAF moonlight raid on March 28, 1942. The city's Museum of Natural History stands gutted in the foreground. British fire bombs destroyed nearly all of Lübeck's largely wooden medieval precinct—a taste of more widespread raids to come.

in fact, had been ordered to post signs on their walls offering second and third helpings of potatoes without extra charge. But by late 1941 even potatoes, the staff of life for the average German, became hard to find. Although the crop had been abundant, much of it was left in the ground because so many farm workers had been drafted into the armed services. A sudden cold snap froze and ruined a large part of what had been harvested. The shipment to market of what remained was erratic because of the continuing dearth of freight cars, most of which were being used to provision troops in the East.

As a result, weeks went by in German cities without the arrival of a single potato. When a shipment did arrive, the ration allowed only four and a half pounds per person a week—a pittance, given the dire shortages of other kinds of food. People complained to the food officials, but to no avail. The government could do little except make false promises of better days to come and give gratuitous tips on how to cope. Through its newspapers, the regime urged citizens not to peel potatoes before boiling them, since this wasted 15 per cent of each tuber; potatoes, so the advice went, should be eaten skin and all. Though sound, such counsel was woefully inadequate. And the German people, who had grown used to feeling slightly hungry, now began to feel the pangs of true hunger.

It did not take long for nutritional deficiencies to affect the health, the appearance and the outlook of the nation. Howard K. Smith, the American correspondent based in Berlin, noted the changes wrought by hunger: "People's faces are pale, unhealthily white as flour, except for red rings around their eyes. One might get accustomed to their faces after a while and think them normal and natural but for the fact that one notices the marked contrast between the young men in uniform, who eat food with vitamins in it and live out of doors part of the time, and the un-uniformed millions who get no vitamins and work in shops and factories 10 to 12 hours a day.

"From lack of vitamins in food," Smith continued, "teeth are decaying fast—my dentist said they are decaying all at once like cubes of sugar dissolving in water. And this winter there has been the most severe epidemic of colds in Berlin; doctors predict it will get worse each year and probably assume dangerous proportions if something cannot be done about food and clothing, especially shoes, which are wearing out fast."

The mood of the people, Smith observed, was deteriorating at the same rate as their health. "It is morbid the way people with weary deadpan faces can flash in an instant into flaming apoplectic fury over some triviality or imaginary insult. You could watch people's natures change as the War proceeded; watch bitterness grow as the end of the War appeared to recede from sight, just as you watch a weed grow. Partly it's the jitters, but mostly it is because people are sick—just plain sick in body and mind."

While the Germans struggled against all odds to maintain a normal life, they were being subjected with increasing frequency to Allied bombing. The Royal Air Force had been dropping bombs on the Reich at intervals since the summer of 1940, but these early raids, carried out at night and aimed at Germany's war industries, often hit nothing. Although city residents were irritated by the warning sirens, the repeated trips to the cellar and the loss of sleep, most did not fear for their lives, for the raids claimed very few civilian casualties.

By the early months of 1942, however, British bombers—and later American bombers as well—were arriving over Germany with growing regularity, and their increased accuracy claimed more and more civilian lives. Then an event occurred that shook the homeland. On the night of the 28th of March, 234 Royal Air Force bombers honed in on the strategic port of Lübeck, in northern Germany. Using a new technique called saturation bombing, they dropped 300 tons of explosives and incendiaries. Lübeck had been founded in medieval times, and most of its buildings were made of wood; it burned like a torch—the first German city to go up in flames. Its destruction sent a shudder of foreboding through the Reich. The German people, whose lives had become a bad dream, now faced a nightmare: For the rest of the War they would be as vulnerable to sudden death as any soldier at the front.

THE EMERGENT HAUSFRAU

A woman aircraft worker wires the ignition system of a new Messerschmitt-109 fighter plane. German women proved to be adept at such intricate jobs.

"WE MUST SERVE WHEREVER WE CAN"

"You help, too!" declares a poster urging women on the home front to aid their fighting men by volunteering for factory, hospital and farm work.

Most of Germany's 14 million working women in 1939 were unpaid hands on family farms or bottom-level workers in industry. When the War began, some middle- and upper-class women took on such previously male jobs as managing post offices and conducting on railroads. But they were exceptions. To the old German adage that a woman's realm was *Kinder, Kirche, Küche* (children, church, kitchen), the Nazis added another. "The female bird pretties herself for her mate and hatches the eggs for him," said Joseph Goebbels, while the man "wards off the enemy."

By 1941, the Nazis had to reconsider. Seven million men were in military service, and the only way to sustain the war effort was to put more women to work. The government launched a recruiting campaign called "Women Help Win the War." Posters, pamphlets and speeches by Nazi leaders now stressed that in taking a job, a woman was simply extending her natural sphere. "It has always been our chief article of faith," declared an official of the Nazi Women's League, "that a woman's place is in the home. But since the whole of Germany is our home, we must serve her wherever we can." The response was lukewarm or worse. When authorities in Dresden invited 1,250 women to a meeting designed to entice them into factory work, a mere 120 signed on for jobs.

By 1943, the number of working men on the home front had sunk to 15 million, less than two thirds of the prewar figure. The government tried to compensate by calling up three million women between the ages of 17 and 45 for factory work. Most of these managed to avoid conscription (fragile health and young children in the home were the surest excuses), and local officials did not enforce the call-up. As a result, the total number of women workers never rose much above the prewar level, although the shift to war-related industrial jobs—and increased responsibility—was substantial. Even then, the tradition of women's dedication to their menfolk refused to die. "Earlier I buttered bread for him," said one soldier's mother. "Now I paint grenades and think, 'This is for him.'"

Signaling through a cloud of steam, a woman works as a train conductor—one of the first jobs women took on as German manpower began to dwindle.

AN ARMY OF FEMALES TO WORK THE FARMS

For many women, war work meant long, exhausting days of farm labor. Rural women had to take up the slack when their husbands and sons left for the Army. Food was such a critical problem for the nation that, beginning in 1939, many thousands of women between the ages of 17 and 25 did a year's duty working on a farm as part of the National Labor Service program. They lived in barracks and marched Army-style to the fields, where they put in 7- to 15-hour stints.

For city girls, farm life was tough. Melita Maschmann, a 17-year-old Berliner, wrote of rubbing her hands raw doing the camp laundry and straining her back planting potatoes. But she was buoyed by a sense that she was serving her country. "I knew the farmers needed us," she said, "and I had come intending not to spare myself."

Shouldering rakes and hoes as though they were firearms, a corps of girls marches to the fields. The five million women and girls working on farms in 1939 dwindled in number as jobs opened up in towns and cities.

As her little girl looks on, a farm wife mucks out the barnyard with the help of a small son clad in his absent father's hat and boots. During the war years, half of all farm work in Germany was carried out by women.

A Red Cross worker offers refreshments to soldiers at a railway station in 1939. Most towns provided free soup and coffee to servicemen passing through.

VOLUNTEERS FOR COMPASSIONATE DUTY

Practically no woman objected to helping the war effort so long as her role was a traditionally feminine one such as nursing or cooking. The Nazi Women's League assured its two million members that such duties were very important. "Though our weapon is only the ladle, its impact will be no less than that of other weapons," declared Gertrude Scholtz-Klink, the leader of the league.

Opportunities abounded for traditional service. Combat-bound servicemen were moving by train and by truck through the nation's cities and villages; soon wounded men were returning to home-front hospitals. German women were prepared for them; some 300,000 donned Red Cross arm bands and stood ready to give the soldiers tender care.

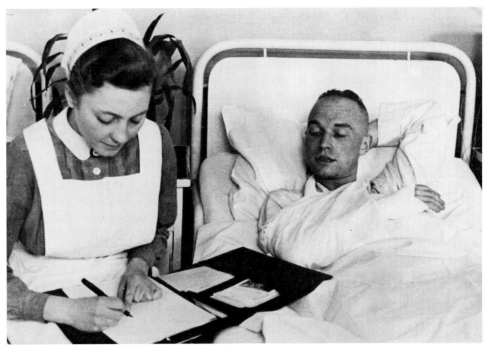

At the bedside of a wounded soldier, a Red Cross nurse takes dictation for a letter home.

A nurse takes a boatload of pajama-clad German servicemen—among them a rank-conscious officer wearing his uniform jacket—for a therapeutic row.

OVERCOMING "FEAR OF THE FACTORY"

The 1943 decree that conscripted women for work in German aircraft, arms and ammunition plants met at first with a reluctant response. One newspaper described the reaction as a new disease: "fear of the factory."

To help women to overcome their apprehensions, the government encouraged plant owners in a number of innovations. A special agency was created to see that factories were made reasonably comfortable and safe. By law, women were exempted from carrying heavy loads. Some factories planted gardens where women could lounge during breaks. Many others introduced training programs in which experienced women workers helped newcomers learn their jobs.

Although a 56-hour work week had become common in German war industry, some employers instituted shorter shifts for married women. The government opened facilities for child care; by 1944 Germany had 32,000 nurseries for the 1.2 million children whose mothers had gone to work.

The liberated ideas that German working women inevitably acquired were symbolized by their attire. For practicality's sake they began wearing slacks—much to the dismay of many German men. One Army officer at Garmisch-Partenkirchen in Bavaria forbade his men to be seen in the company of "trouser women." His order was overruled by Propaganda Minister Goebbels, who recognized that such old-fashioned scruples could undermine the distaff contribution to the War. "Whether women wear trousers is no concern of the public," he declared. "The bigotry bug should be wiped out."

A Bonn woman punches a factory time clock.

In an aircraft plant, a woman installs part of an instrument panel. Women also helped to manufacture ships, tanks, cannon, grenades and ammunition.

Inside the uncompleted fuselage of a Luftwaffe bomber, a woman aircraft worker balances on a protective pad as she rivets a member into place overhead.

Women assemble 88mm shell fuses at a munitions factory. The pay of women workers increased as labor grew scarce; but it remained below men's wages.

An experienced welder steadies a trainee's hands. A program of women teaching women turned out thousands of skilled workers, despite male skepticism.

PERILOUS ASSIGNMENTS IN UNIFORM

By 1944, there was such a shortage of German manpower that women moved into quasi-military jobs. That October the government issued a call for 100,000 women to staff antiaircraft teams. Though not admitted to the armed forces, they were allowed to wear military insignia, and they learned to operate searchlights, detection instruments and communications installations during Allied bombing raids.

The work was painstaking and nerve-racking. "One small error in concentration in taking a report or transmission could have dire consequences, yes, in some instances even cost lives," one such flak helper said of her job.

By 1945, as Germany made its desperate last-ditch defense against the Allied assault, women even took over antiaircraft guns. Some shot down Allied bombers, and many sacrificed their lives.

Under the tutelage of a Luftwaffe airman, flak helpers learn how to recognize a B-17 bomber.

Wearing earphones that are wired to a bowl-shaped sound detector, two women antiaircraft helpers listen for enemy planes while a soldier coaches them.

Two seated women learn to manipulate the control board of an aircraft searchlight while a third perches on the side to track a target and a fourth looks on.

Wearing helmets during an air raid, military auxiliaries handle a hectic switchboard relaying messages between antiaircraft stations.

Transcribing information they have received from a network of spotters, Luftwaffe flak helpers chart on a plotting board the course of incoming enemy bombers.

Two women, silhouetted against a glaring searchlight, attempt to locate enemy aircraft overhead with a direction indicator, an instrument that determined range and altitude.

FLAK: THE PROTECTIVE WALL

A 1942 painting portrays the crew of a 37mm antiaircraft gun scanning the skies over a factory town in the Ruhr valley for a glimpse of incoming planes.

ON CONSTANT VIGIL WITH 20,000 GUNS

As ubiquitous as the gabled housetops and factory chimneys they protected, the antiaircraft batteries of the Luftwaffe became such a familiar feature of the wartime landscape, an observer in the Ruhr valley wrote in 1942, that "the laborers on their way to work and travelers looking out of train windows no longer notice them."

The Germans called these weapons *Flak,* an acronym for *Fliegerabwehrkanonen,* or antiaircraft guns. The million-odd Luftwaffe artillerymen and auxiliaries trained to operate them went into instant action when a warning was received that Allied bombers were on the way. At the same time sausage-like barrage balloons—nicknamed rubber flak—were winched upward on their tethers to surround factories and railyards with a curtain of steel cables. Saucer-shaped radar rotated northward and westward to probe the sky for approaching enemy planes, their motions followed by the gigantic reflector drums of swivel-mounted searchlights. The antiaircraft guns themselves—20,693 of them, spaced throughout Germany's western regions—ranged from slender-barreled 20mm automatics that fired 4-ounce bullets to ponderous 128mm cannon that could hurl a 57-pound high-explosive shell to an altitude of 35,000 feet. Their destructive fire made "flak" a word that Allied aircrews came to fear.

By December 1942 the flak units had claimed 8,706 enemy aircraft. But not even this awesome score could sustain Luftwaffe chief Hermann Göring's boast of August 1939 that "not a single bomb" would ever fall on the Ruhr. During 1942, the RAF and the U.S. Army Air Forces scarred the industrial centers of Germany with 53,755 tons of bombs in spite of the best efforts of the Luftwaffe's air and ground defenders.

Perhaps to evoke public sympathy for the hard-pressed flak detachments, the general who commanded the Ruhr's air defenses commissioned a book of drawings and paintings by talented flak artillerymen. The reproductions on these pages are from that book and from the work of other German soldier-artists.

An artilleryman focuses a range finder. When images from lenses at each end of the tube merged, calibrations on the glass gave the target distance.

A gun commander wearing headphones (right) receives range information as three loaders (center) set the next round's fuse by the light of the muzzle flash.

A ground crew adjusts the mooring lines of one of the 1,625 hydrogen-filled barrage balloons that surrounded prime industrial targets in the Ruhr and Rhine valleys and such port cities as Hamburg and Bremen. The steel mooring cables thwarted low-flying bombers.

A square of antiaircraft guns guards factories along the Rhine River near Oberhausen. Vegetable gardens (foreground) provided a productive off-duty diversion for the gun crews.

At a field bunker, a Luftwaffe enlisted man prepares to use his 10 x 80 spotting telescope to locate approaching bombers. Later, after casualties and transfers reduced the gun crews, women and boys took over this task.

93

A painting by a German sergeant, entitled "Alarm in the Battery," shows a gun crew racing to action stations near Münster under a full moon—called a bomber's moon because it helped to illuminate targets.

Sunset brings the crew members of a searchlight battery to the alert in an emplacement near Cologne. Some 4,200 searchlights, spaced three miles apart in chessboard patterns around German cities, "coned" their beams to illuminate enemy bombers—and, incidentally, blind the bombardiers.

An orchestration of fire and light greets RAF bombers over Hamburg on July 25, 1943. Shells from dual-mounted 128mm guns (right) burst around a lead bomber coned by searchlights, tracer bullets curve upward, and multicolored British "Christmas tree" flares descend toward the city.

95

3

Beginning in August 1942, Germans at home avidly followed the progress of the Wehrmacht as it beseiged and then penetrated the Russian metropolis of Stalingrad in bitter house-to-house fighting. Press dispatches received from the front were displayed prominently, and Germans became obsessed with the battle. They saw it, one newspaper reported, as the "crucial cornerstone" of a campaign that would bring the nation final victory.

But suddenly the campaign, which had assumed almost magical significance, turned sour. In mid-November the Red Army launched a million-man counteroffensive and rapidly encircled the German Sixth Army of General Friedrich von Paulus. The news reports grew vague, but it was beyond concealment that Paulus' 300,000 men were freezing and starving in an ever-tightening pocket. By January of 1943 even the most optimistic Germans had written off the Sixth Army as lost.

To explain the stunning turnabout at Stalingrad, Hitler ordered Nazi Party leaders in cities across the country to deliver speeches that he hoped would stiffen the national will. One of these preachers for the party was Paul Giesler, who was Gauleiter, or district leader, of Bavaria and the holder of an honor badge in gold for his earlier service as a Storm Troop leader. Giesler took as his special target the students of the University of Munich. At the spacious auditorium of the German Museum of Technology—one of the few halls in Munich that was large enough for the purpose—he assembled the university's faculty and student body of 4,000 on January 13, 1943.

While Gestapo agents and SS men stood guard at the exits, Giesler began his speech with a somber recounting of the situation at Stalingrad. He sought to place the blame for the sudden reversal on the German people in general and on the students in particular—a view he ascribed to Hitler himself. The Führer, Giesler explained, had no use for youths who buried their heads in books. He accused the young men of using their studies to evade military service. They were malingerers, he said, and all who could go into the Army or work in war industries would soon be called up to do so.

"As for the girls," Giesler went on, "they have healthy bodies; let them bear children. There is no reason why every girl student should not for each of her years at the uni-

VOICES OF DISSENT

versity present an annual testimonial in the form of a son.

"I realize," Giesler continued with a suggestive snigger, "that a certain amount of cooperation is required, and if some of the girls lack sufficient charm to find a mate, I will assign to each of them one of my adjutants, whose antecedents I can vouch for; and I can promise her a thoroughly enjoyable experience."

At this point Giesler was interrupted. "We won't have our fellow students insulted!" shouted a voice from the audience—and in an instant the hall was in an uproar. Students rushed the Gestapo and SS guards and threw some of them down the stairs. Several students were arrested. Many others surged out into the streets, where a spontaneous demonstration erupted. Linking arms, the students marched defiantly through the middle of the city. Singing and shouting, the students cried, "Free our comrades! Give us back our comrades!" For several hours the demonstration went on, until the Munich Riot Police arrived and waded into the students with clubs flailing.

SS chief Heinrich Himmler was outraged when he heard of the episode. He declared a state of emergency in Munich, and to prevent news of the demonstration from spreading, he ordered telephone and radio service cut off and forbade any mention of the incident in the press. Despite these measures, word of the student uprising drifted across the Reich. Smaller—but equally heartfelt—student protests followed over the next few weeks in Frankfurt, Stuttgart and the Ruhr.

Such demonstrations were but one indication that not all Germans were marching in lock step to Hitler's tune. Simmering under the surface of his seemingly cohesive and obedient society was a foment compounded of disillusionment, dismay and discontent. The feeling seldom erupted so dramatically as at the University of Munich, but everywhere in Germany there were quieter manifestations of a subdued but undeniable resistance to the state of affairs Hitler's regime had wrought. Some of it simply reflected war weariness. But much of it was generated by the late-dawning realization that Hitler's promises were not being fulfilled—and that the repressive measures he had instituted were uncivilized and intolerable.

The resistance took many forms. At its most innocuous, it consisted of *Flüsterwitze,* whispered jokes, so called because Germans were careful not to recount them aloud. One such joke went: "Do you know that in the future teeth are going to be pulled through the nose?" "Why?" "Because nobody dares open his mouth." According to another, three good fairies were present at Hitler's birth. The first wished that every German should be honest, the second that every German should be intelligent, and the third that every German should be a National Socialist. Then a bad fairy appeared. She ordered that every German should possess only two of the three attributes. So the Führer was left with intelligent Nazis who were not honest; honest Nazis who were not intelligent; and honest, intelligent citizens who were not Nazis.

Not all the reaction took the form of jokes. At the other extreme were acts of violence and sabotage. In Cologne, a group of iconoclastic students who called themselves the Edelweiss Pirates sheltered Army deserters and actually clashed with the police—one of the few instances of armed insurrection inside the Reich.

Between the extremes was action of another kind: Many Germans engaged in courageous efforts to sway the minds of the people through the written word, and through sermons from many pulpits urging the faithful to resist the Nazis' assaults on freedom of religion. In addition, there was passive resistance from thousands of German citizens who never came to the notice of the authorities—from Jews who had eluded Nazi repression, and from gentiles who had helped them do so. Indeed, recalled Rabbi Leo Baeck, the venerable leader of Berlin's Jewish community, "sometimes the only way Germans could express their opposition to the Nazis was to be helpful to a Jew."

No people in Germany suffered more under Hitler's regime than the Jews. For complex reasons lying deep in his psyche, Hitler had had an irrational aversion to Jews ever since his youth in Vienna—a polyglot city where ethnic groups from all over Eastern Europe congregated, but where those of Germanic stock were the ruling class. He had given expression to that aversion as far back as 1924, when he wrote his political testament, *Mein Kampf.* In the book he fulminated that if 15,000 "Hebrew corrupters" of the nation had been eliminated with poison gas in 1914, millions of German lives might have been spared in the First World War.

Within a few months of taking power in 1933, the Nazis had begun to make life difficult for Germany's Jews. The Gestapo drew up lists of all persons who were Jewish—district by district—and all such persons were required to carry identification cards stamped with a large *J* for *Jude*, or Jew. Soon after, the government issued a decree calling for a boycott of Jewish businesses—and Nazi Storm Troopers formed picket lines to enforce the boycott with their fists.

American journalist Albion Ross decided to see what would happen if he crossed one of the Nazi picket lines. He marched resolutely into a Jewish-owned department store, bought a small item from a startled clerk and headed out the door. The brown-shirted Nazi guards enforcing the boycott were ready for him. "Before I knew what was happening," Ross recalled, "blows were raining down on me. I ran. They followed, beating me over the head and back."

Ross managed to outdistance his assailants, who evidently were under orders not to stray too far from the picket lines. The picketing lasted only a few days and had little lasting effect on Jewish businesses, many of which, ironically, prospered under the Nazi-sparked economic renaissance. Only a few thousand Jews recognized the boycotts for what they were—the beginning of a savage persecution that eventually led to the slaughter of millions—and emigrated. Most clung doggedly to the hope that the Nazi terror would abate.

In fact, the picket lines were only the beginning. Shortly thereafter, the Nazis stripped the Jews of German citizenship, removed them from professional and civil-service positions and forbade them to use public facilities. On November 9, 1938, the government used the assassination of a German diplomat in Paris by a Jewish refugee as an excuse to incite rioting in cities all over Germany. In one terrible night, rampaging Nazi thugs burned and looted thousands of Jewish businesses and smashed so much window glass that the episode came to be known as *Kristallnacht*, or Crystal Night.

In the wake of Crystal Night, the trickle of Jews leaving the Reich became a torrent; by July 1940, a total of 280,000 German and 140,000 Austrian Jews had emigrated. For the 200,000 Jews who remained, the repression grew relentlessly worse. When Allied bombing of German cities began, the Jews were made to seek safety in segregated shelters—and the ones available to them were woefully inadequate. "We were in the basement room with the hot-water pipes," said one man, "so if there had been a direct hit we would have been killed first. If the bombs didn't get us, then the hot water would." Sometimes, he added, the Jews prayed for a direct hit that would also kill the Nazis sheltered below them.

German Jews literally became marked people in September 1941, when the government decreed that every Jew must identify himself by wearing a yellow, six-pointed star marked *Jude*. A short time later the Nazis began deporting them under a program explained as "resettlement." The undertaking began abruptly and without explanation; in Berlin, the Gestapo appeared at the Levetzowstrasse synagogue after services for Yom Kippur—the holiest of the Jewish holidays—and announced that the building would be the staging site for the deportation of Berlin's 35,000 remaining Jews. The worshippers in the synagogue that night were ordered to report "with bedding and rations for five days" for resettlement in the East; other Jews were mailed a notice that said simply, "Prepare to be evacuated." Similar occurrences took place all over Germany. By 1943 Jewish shops were closed everywhere, and apartments where Jewish families had lived stood empty.

The legend on this cartoon, posted surreptitiously in public places in 1943 and 1944, urges Germans to "destroy the tyrant before it is too late." Anti-Nazi propagandists also distributed leaflets disguised as timetables, city maps, theater programs and even as official Nazi publications.

The spectacle of the Jews' departure left an indelible picture in the memories of those who witnessed it. A young German boy who watched in the Moselle township of Wittlich—which had a Jewish population of 50—remembered that the Jews were driven away "packed together in two trucks" toward the nearest railhead. "I thought they were going to be resettled in Poland or somewhere like that," the boy later remembered. "I thought it was cruel to uproot old people like that, but I didn't suspect what was really going to happen."

Word of what was really happening trickled out to the general public only slowly. Little by little—here from an indiscreet party leader, there from a soldier on leave from the East—Germans began to hear rumors that the Jews were not being resettled; they were being systematically murdered in concentration camps. Many Germans found the stories difficult to believe. One young woman recalled her father's astonished reaction when a highly placed Nazi told him similar stories about the concentration camps. "You must be joking," said the father. "Germans would not do such things." A Berlin writer named Ruth Andreas-Friedrich, who eventually helped many Jews to hide, wrote of the rumors in her diary: " 'They are forced to dig their own graves,' people whisper. 'Their clothing, shoes, shirts are taken from them. They are sent naked to their deaths.' The horror is so incredible that the imagination refuses to accept its reality."

About 140,000 German Jews all told were sent to concentration camps, and some 90 per cent of them died there as part of the Nazi purge that ultimately claimed more than five million Jewish lives throughout Europe.

In 1944, SS chief Himmler declared Berlin to be *Judenrein*—"clean of Jews." He was wrong. In Berlin and in other large cities, some Jews had gone into hiding when they first learned of the deportations and the death camps; they came to be known as "U-boats" because they lived submerged. Others, reluctant to give up what few creature comforts remained to them, waited where they were—fearful but stubborn, wondering with every knock on the door whether the Gestapo had come to fetch them. Some Jews masqueraded as Aryans; others managed to go right on celebrating their holy days without being detected. Some lived by their own wits; others survived with the conniv-ance of gentiles who refused to give them away. A rare few managed to find jobs.

For the Jews who hid, every day was harrowing—a steady regimen, one said, of "flight and hunger and fear." Moves were frequent simply because there was a need to avoid the glances of curious neighbors. Food was scarce because two or three people often had to live on one gentile friend's ration card. Travel was nerve-racking since identity checks were conducted repeatedly and exhaustively, and few Jews had papers that would allow them to pass as Aryans. Even so, an estimated 5,000 Berlin Jews managed to survive in the very eye of the deadly storm swirling about them. For them—and for the Germans who helped and hid them—every day of survival was an act of resistance.

Typical of the Jews who went into hiding was Erich Hopp, a Berlin writer. Hopp, his wife, Charlotte, and their 14-year-old son, Wolfgang, had lived a comfortable middle-class existence that little prepared them for what was to come. One evening in May 1942, the Hopps found in their mailbox a notice from the Gestapo ordering them to be ready for deportation in two days. The three sat up all night weighing their chances for survival. "If we avoided deportation," Hopp remembered thinking, "how could we get along without a place to live, without food ration cards, always in danger of being reported by self-appointed denouncers? But deportation meant at best a precarious living and perhaps death." So the Hopps decided to submerge.

The Hopps's priority, in the two days' grace they had been given to wrap up their affairs, was to find shelter. Erich Hopp asked several friends for help; he was rejected wherever he turned. Some of the reasons he was given were patently absurd: One man declined, Hopp said, because "our Jewish corpses might be found in his apartment after an air raid." Charlotte Hopp had better luck; she found a sympathetic woman who agreed to hide the family in the Mulackstrasse, Berlin's red-light district. "We did not expect to live well," Erich Hopp later recalled. "We only wanted to live." After leaving a phony suicide note requesting that they be buried together when their bodies were found, the Hopps scuttled under cover of darkness to their first refuge—a brothel. They lived there for 10 days, then decided they had better seek a shelter less open to public scrutiny.

Poised at their instruments, student musicians from the Jewish Youth Orchestra of Berlin listen as conductor Max Wolheim instructs them on the playing of a passage.

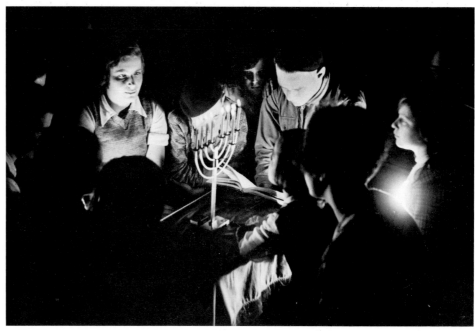

Celebrating Hanukkah in December 1939, children in a Jewish youth center in Berlin gather around a fully lighted Menorah to hear the eldest boy read prayers on the eighth and last night of the religious holiday.

A PHOTOGRAPHER'S LOG OF SEGREGATED BERLIN

Following the vicious Crystal Night rampage against German Jews on November 9, 1938, the Nazis forced the few remaining Jewish newspapers in Berlin to share a single photographer. He was Abraham Pisarek, the official photographer of the Jewish Cultural Association and an authority on traditional Jewish customs.

Pisarek had not escaped Crystal Night unscathed: His studio was raided by thugs who smashed equipment and confiscated photographs. But his cameras survived, and he kept on taking pictures, amassing a visual record of the Jews' struggle to maintain their culture despite Nazi oppression.

Pisarek photographed Jewish musicians and actors performing popular German music and plays, Jewish athletes competing in segregated all-Jewish events, Jews worshipping, and Jewish émigrés learning new languages and trades to take to America or Palestine. He also risked his life to photograph surreptitiously the funeral of a Jewish artist, Max Liebermann, whom the Nazis had termed "degenerate" and wanted buried without notice.

In 1941, the Nazis dissolved the Jewish Cultural Association and confiscated the contents of the Jewish Museum, including Pisarek's pictures. Pisarek was forced to surrender his cameras and to labor in factories for the next four years.

When freed by the Red Army in 1945, Pisarek, who spoke Russian, found work as an interpreter. One day Soviet officers told him they had come upon a room in an abandoned building filled with art from the Jewish Museum. There Pisarek found two large boxes—and in them many of the photographs he had given up for lost.

Sprinting around a turn, Jewish athletes compete in a 400-meter relay in Berlin's Jewish sports field in 1938. A runner wearing his team's Star-of-David emblem leads the race.

Unable to find a place that would take them in together, they were forced to separate.

Erich Hopp found refuge with a cousin's gentile widow, who hid him in a narrow little room in her apartment in Lichtenberg, an eastern suburb of Berlin. "I did not leave the apartment for 21 months," Hopp later recalled. He slept on a sofa "so small that I had to curl up like a question mark. Instead of talking I had to whisper; and when I walked I had to tiptoe. The room was cold, and for exercise I walked its length, a distance of about 12 feet, 25 times."

Charlotte and Wolfgang, meanwhile, embarked on a gypsy-like existence, staying a week here, a week there. When confronted by inquisitive strangers, they explained their presence by saying they had been bombed out of their home and had lost their papers. The chaos that Allied bombing had brought to Germany enabled many other Jews to use the same excuse to survive. But Charlotte found the gypsy life too precarious for her teen-age son; after a few months she sent Wolfgang to move in with his father and share his cramped existence. She found shelter for herself with an elderly professor who lived in Eichwalde, a town southeast of Berlin. "At last she had a real home," her husband later wrote, "and could devote herself to the task of getting food for her family."

The task was a formidable one; the Hopps had thrown away their telltale ration cards and identification papers. Charlotte used a blank sheet of Propaganda Ministry stationery signed by Joseph Goebbels himself—and given to her by a friend—to forge an official-looking travel pass. With it, she felt free to move about the city. Then she drew up a list of people who might each be able to spare a bit of food. Soon she had a weekly schedule, getting a few bits of bread from one person, a pat of margarine or some moldy potatoes from another; scraps of horse meat and fat were a luxury. With those pathetic offerings, Charlotte Hopp faithfully delivered food to her husband and son, week after week. Seldom was she able to spend much time with them, but for the rest of the War—another three years—she kept them alive with her artful scavenging.

Alice Stein-Landesmann, a novelist who went underground in October 1942, had a different means of survival. She hid in the apartment of a gentile friend and survived by discarding the manners of the cosmopolitan intellectual she was and adopting those of a lower-middle-class *Hausfrau*, blending into the crowd. "I adapted myself to the district in which I lived just as animals instinctively blend into their surroundings," she later recounted. "I wore no hat and no rings, went shopping wearing an apron and fell into the habit of speaking carelessly. I was never regarded with suspicion."

Hans Rosenthal, who would become a popular entertainer in Germany after the War, survived by masquerading as a gentile and found work as a gravedigger. On one occasion he had to dig graves for two high-ranking SS officers. "I told myself," he later recalled, "that I probably was the only Jew in Germany putting Nazis under the earth."

Joel König, who once had marched in a torchlight parade to celebrate Hitler's rise to power—like many Jews, he failed at first to recognize what the Nazis had in store—secured false papers in 1942 and worked in a plant that manufactured electrical parts for submarines. By the spring of 1943, König had come to regard his own submerged existence as too oppressive and was desperate to escape Germany. Needing help, he admitted to his supervisor, an engineer named Helmut Krell, that he was a Jew. Krell was appalled. "You realize of course," he replied, "you are like an unexploded bomb now that you have let me know." Nevertheless, Krell went on, "it is my duty as a human being to help you escape." He arranged for König to make a business trip to Hungary, which, though allied to Germany, had been relatively lenient in its treatment of Jews. There, in Budapest, Joel König survived; he managed to emigrate to Palestine in 1944.

Valerie Wolffenstein, a painter who had been baptized and brought up as a Protestant but was considered a Jew by the Nazis because her father was Jewish, moved 18 times in little more than two years to avoid detection. "Each time I moved," she remembered, "I was tormented anew with fear of discovery on the trip and of unknown dangers in my new refuge. Often I did not know until just before my departure what new asylum had been found for me." In one instance, a friend who was trying to find a place for her with a farm family named Gasteiger notified her that the quest had succeeded by sending her a postcard saying "Farmer

G.'s wife will take one of the two puppies, the plump one with the brown eyes." It was, she noted wryly, "an excellent description of me."

Valerie Wolffenstein's odyssey was typical of the way many German Jews managed to evade the authorities: They were passed from one German to another in a kind of underground railroad. "There were still enough Germans," recalled the anti-Nazi gentile Ruth Andreas-Friedrich, "who held it an honor to snap their fingers at the Jewish laws." She became a member of a Berlin group that took the code name *Uncle Emil* and specialized in helping Jews. Its members, who numbered about two dozen, included doctors, professors, actors, writers and other professionals. Among the most important of them was a master printer. Another member recalled that he could "forge to perfection almost anything in the way of a needed official document such as a pass, a military-exemption certificate or a strip of food tickets to feed a famished Jew."

A hideout, said Ruth Andreas-Friedrich, "was a gift from heaven. The gang moved these guests from one to another. 'You take them one night, we'll take them the next.' Permanent guests were suspicious looking. The constant coming and going made the neighbors mistrustful, anyway."

The Jews who elected to live underground rather than flee had little idea what lay ahead. "If we had known then," recalled Rolf Joseph, who with his brother Alfred had resisted deportation, "that this existence would last three long years, I don't think we would have had the courage to go on. But we were young and were kept going by our deep hatred of the Nazis and, I suppose, by a sense of adventure."

The Joseph brothers had made a rope ladder to drop from their third-floor room to the cemetery bordering their apartment building if the Gestapo came to take them away. But they did not have an opportunity to use it. On June 6, 1942, Rolf, then 21, was returning home from his job in a furniture factory late in the afternoon when he noticed a furniture van in front of his home. "A neighbor waved to me to go away," Rolf remembered, "but I could not go. I ran up the stairs and listened at the apartment door. I heard my mother crying and a strange man shouting at her." Only then did Rolf realize that the Gestapo had come to deport his

family, and now he took the neighbor's advice. "In a panic I rushed down the stairs. I ran through the streets until I was out of breath."

Rolf Joseph never saw his mother again. But by inquiring of one friend after another, he did find his brother, who was staying with a family in Oranienburg, a northern suburb of Berlin. The refuge proved only temporary; the hosts feared for their own safety, and after a few days asked the brothers to leave. For the next four months, Rolf and Alfred had no shelter, but simply wandered around Berlin in the pleasant summer weather or rode in the streetcars or the subway until late at night. "We always were in fear of being stopped to show our identification cards with the large *J* on them," Rolf related. "We spent nights in parks and woods, and when the weather was very bad, in railway station washrooms."

Eventually, Rolf and Alfred Joseph found refuge with a woman they knew as Frau Mieze, an amiable old eccentric, in her junk-cluttered house in Berlin's Tegelerstrasse, a picturesque wooded area north of the city. Then the mother of a gentile friend who had died gave Rolf Joseph her son's identity card, which was not stamped with the telltale *J*. As "Paul Wagner," Rolf was able to wander the streets of Berlin safely for several weeks. But one day two military policemen stopped him near a railway station; they apparently suspected him of being a deserter since most able-bodied men in Germany were in military service. After examining his identity card, they arrested him; the name Paul Wagner was indeed on their list of German AWOLs.

At the nearest police station, Rolf revealed himself as a Jew; it was safer to do that than to risk immediate execution as a deserter. He was imprisoned and interrogated by the Gestapo. "Time and time again they demanded the names of the people who were sheltering me," he recalled, "but I refused. Then they tied my hands and feet, strapped me on a wooden box and gave me 25 lashes with a horsewhip on my naked buttocks. The physical pain was bad, but worse still was the fact that these criminals had the power to humiliate me. It strengthened my determination not to let them break my spirit."

Together with five fellow prisoners, Rolf made two attempts to escape; each time they were recaptured and brutally beaten. The second beating gave Rolf the means for a third escape attempt. "I was struck in the face with a whip," he related. "Suddenly body and mind revolted, and I developed a high fever. The fever gave me an idea. I knew the SS were afraid of contagious diseases, so I scratched myself up badly and said I had scarlet fever."

Strange to say, the SS doctor confirmed Rolf's diagnosis and sent him to a prison hospital. There he talked a sympathetic nurse into giving him a pair of trousers, and—with a lever made of a wet towel and a piece of wood—he managed to widen the space between two bars in the window of his third-floor cell enough to slip through. "It was a leap into uncertainty," he said later, "but it might lead to freedom. I hit the ground with a terrible thud and a shooting pain went through my spine. I felt as if I were paralyzed, but fear kept me moving. I climbed over the prison wall and managed to leap onto a passing streetcar. No one paid any attention to my strange attire—maybe they thought I was bombed out."

Rolf got off the streetcar at Tegelerstrasse and made his way to Frau Mieze's ramshackle house, where he rejoined his brother and the old woman. For the next three months they ministered to him while he lay on a mattress of stacked newspapers, barely able to move because of the injuries he had suffered in his fall. Finally, he felt strong enough to scrounge around Berlin for food. One day he ran into a man with whom he had once worked as a carpenter. The man, Jakob Post, who knew Rolf was Jewish, invited him to come back to his apartment on the following day for some food. Post welcomed him warmly, then asked him to wait while he ran an errand.

Rolf Joseph had been too trusting. When his host returned, he was with two members of the police. "This time there seemed no way out," Rolf recalled, "and I was too weak physically and mentally to offer resistance. They asked no questions, for Post had told them all they needed to know. I had to walk between them to the police station. We had gone a short way when I stopped. Hardly realizing what I was doing, I said quietly:

" 'You can do what you like with me. You can shoot me right here. But I am not going with you. I'd rather die right on this street—right now. I've had enough.' "

The two policemen drew their revolvers and cocked them. Rolf stood deadly still, not uttering a word. After perhaps a minute, he had the surprise of his life. One officer turned to the other and whispered, "Shall we let him run?"

"I don't care," answered his partner. Exchanging a few more words, they agreed to let Rolf go free so long as he promised not to let Jakob Post ever lay eyes on him again. "That might make trouble for us," one of the policemen said. Rolf nodded, turned around and walked slowly away. "If I had been able to speak," he said later, "I would have shouted for joy."

Once again he rejoined his brother and Frau Mieze. Her house was eventually bombed by the Allies, but the odd threesome retreated to a plot of land the old woman owned outside Berlin and resumed their hand-to-mouth existence.

Even luckier than Rolf and Alfred Joseph were the Sengers, a Frankfurt family who masqueraded as Aryans so adroitly that the Senger sons, Alex and Valentin, eventually were drafted into the Army. As far as is known, the Sengers—the parents, their two sons and a daughter, Paula—were the only Jewish family to leave a record of their living inside Germany through the War without going underground. To survive in the open, said Valentin Senger, required "a thousand lucky breaks."

The first break occurred in the summer of 1933, the year of Hitler's accession. At that time the Sengers were carrying internal passports marked "stateless" because the parents were refugees from czarist Russia. When the Gestapo ordered all police districts in Germany to draw up lists of persons listed in official files as "Hebraic," a local police sergeant named Kaspar came to the Sengers' house. "He conferred with Mama behind closed doors," Valentin Senger recalled. "He had made inquiries, he told her, and was sure that we would have a hard time of it if our name was put on the list of Jews. Rumors were going around

that Jews would soon be moved into segregated areas and made to pay much higher taxes. And other, still severer measures were thought to be in the offing."

The sergeant's concern for their welfare would mystify the Sengers for the rest of their lives. Whatever the reason, he told the mother, Olga Senger, that he had made "a little change" in the family's registration card, from "Hebraic" to "Nonconformist." Later he did them a further favor; he destroyed the corrected card and replaced it with a new one that showed no signs of having been altered.

The registration card spared the Senger family harassment from the police. But they faced a surprise challenge from young Valentin's school one day when his "racial science" teacher ordered him to draw up a family tree. "Suppose I had come to class with the real family trees of the Rabizano-vitches and Sudakoviches!" he later wrote. Instead, Valentin sat down with his parents, pruned an ancestor here, grafted one on there and came up with a convincing family tree that made his ancestors out to be Volga Germans, who had settled in Russia in the time of Catherine the Great.

A few weeks later, the teacher gave the class another exercise in racial studies. Brandishing calipers, he explained that the instrument could determine race by measuring physiognomy. Valentin Senger was his first guinea pig.

"Applying the arms of his calipers to my head, front and back, left and right, he wrote down figures," Senger later recalled. "He took one chart, then another from his desk, held them up to his thick eyeglasses, wrote figures on the blackboard, added, subtracted, multiplied." When he had finished, the science teacher turned to the class and proclaimed: "Senger, Dinaric type with Eastern admixture. Aryan race, sound to the core."

After Valentin left school, a family friend helped him to get a job as an apprentice draftsman. In 1938, the final year of his apprenticeship, he was working at a steel plant in Sachsenhausen, across the river from Frankfurt. One day he made the mistake of remarking to a fellow worker that Crystal Night had been "un-Christian." The listener turned out to be a Hitler Youth fanatic; he reported him to their supervisor. Once again, Senger's luck held. The supervisor got rid of the problem by having him transferred to another plant, where he eventually became a department head.

The family had a fresh scare in 1940 when Valentin's fa-ther, a skilled lathe operator, went back to work at a small cogwheel factory at the age of 70. Despite his thick Yiddish accent, which he explained as a "Volga dialect," the elder Senger thrived at the factory; his fluency in Russian earned him a job supervising the plant's Russian slave laborers, all of whom were women.

Then on a morning in December 1943 came another fright. The Gestapo arrested Senger and charged him with sabotaging the war effort by coddling the Russian workers. After hours of questioning, the Gestapo released him. His crime, they told him, was that he was "too kindhearted"; he had been led astray, they said, "by false pity for the women in his care." He got off with a warning to be more careful in the future.

The Sengers faced their severest test in the summer of 1944, when Valentin and his brother Alex received draft notices. They feared that the induction physical, by exposing their circumcisions, would be their undoing, but they decided nonetheless to report. "What else could we do?" wrote Valentin Senger. "Fail to show up? They would come and get us. Disappear? But where to? Even if it were possible, our disappearance would lead the authorities to our parents and that would be the end of them."

To their surprise, both Sengers passed the physical with no questions asked. Alex was assigned to infantry training and Valentin to the artillery. Their successful flouting of the Nazis' decrees had earned them a place in the army of the nation that had sought to be rid of them.

Those Germans who ignored the plight of the Jews found out sooner or later that the Nazis had equally harsh treatment in store for many non-Jews. In the autumn of 1940, the readers of a number of German provincial newspapers became aware that the obituary notices had a strange ring about them. Death seemed to occur repeatedly at one of three relatively isolated places—Grafeneck, a lonely castle 60 miles southeast of Stuttgart; Hartheim, a castle near Linz on the Danube River; and Sonnenstein, a public medical and nursing institute at Pirna in Saxony. Furthermore, most of the notices were worded in much the same way. "After weeks of anxious uncertainty," read a typical item, "we received the shocking news on September 18 that our beloved Marianne died of grippe on September 15 at Pirna.

The cremation took place there." What was more, the bereaved families discovered when they compared notes, they invariably received the ashes of the deceased by mail, along with a stern warning from the Gestapo not to demand explanations.

If explanations had been forthcoming, the public would have learned that the Nazis had embarked on a program to exterminate all mentally retarded children and adults under the guise of euthanasia, or mercy killing. The Nazis tried subtly to encourage the acceptance of their deadly program; a film entitled *I Accuse (pages 118-119)*, a tear-jerking melodrama about a physician who administers a lethal overdose of drugs to his incurably ill wife, was part of their pro-euthanasia campaign.

Germans by and large found the prospect of euthanasia dismaying. But like all rumors, those describing the dark deeds allegedly occurring at the castles and the mental hospital aroused more talk than practical action. It took a clergyman to raise the first show of resistance. He was Dr. Friedrich von Bodelschwingh, a Protestant minister widely known and liked in the Westphalian town of Bielefeld, where he ran the Bethel Institute, an asylum for retarded children. In the summer of 1940, he received an order to deliver some of the children to the authorities.

Instinctively, Bodelschwingh feared for the lives of his charges, and he refused to do as he was bidden. Instead he went to Berlin and asked a high-ranking friend to protest to Hitler himself. The protest was to no avail. Back in Bielefeld, he received a visit from the local gauleiter, who ordered him once again to hand over the children. Again

Bodelschwingh refused, and the Gestapo ordered the gauleiter to arrest him.

Now the gauleiter took an unexpected stand. He told the Berlin authorities that Bodelschwingh was the most popular man in the entire province, and that if the Gestapo agents wanted him they would have to arrest him themselves.

Before the Gestapo could act, the asylum was bombed, on September 18, 1940. More than a dozen children died. The Nazis blamed the Royal Air Force for the incident, headlining it "Murder of Children at Bethel—Revolting Crime." Bodelschwingh escaped injury in the raid, and the pressure on him to turn over his young patients eased.

Meanwhile, the euthanasia program was continuing at other institutions—and another clergyman stepped in to protest it. He was Count Clemens von Galen, a hawk-nosed, silver-haired aristocrat who was the Catholic Bishop of Münster. For more than two years, Galen had been smarting over a series of Nazi assaults on church freedoms, among them a ban on religious processions and church collections and the passage of a law that allowed any child over the age of 14 to leave the Church without parental permission.

Galen's fear of even more draconian measures caused him to hold his tongue until May of 1941, when he wrote an open letter to Bishop Wilhelm Berning of Osnabrück saying that it was time "to consider whether this passive resistance forced on us should continue. As Catholic bishops have we not the duty to defend the freedom and the rights of the Church? I ask myself if we should not do more than we have up to now. Is not our holy Church being robbed, repressed

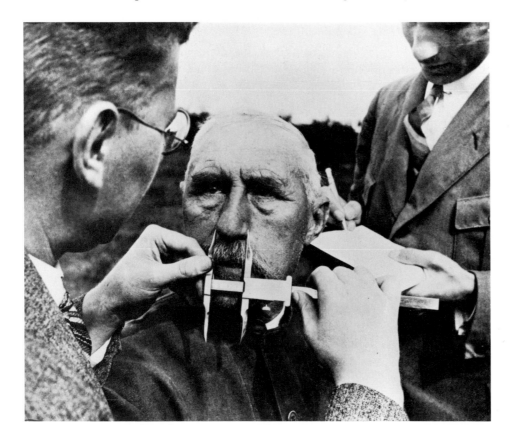

Government officials conduct a racial test on a German of "doubtful origins," using a pair of calipers to measure his nose. The theory behind such humiliating tests equated "proper" facial proportions with Aryan purity.

and gagged, nearly liquidated? Are not priests being locked up without trial simply because they have worked successfully for our holy religion?"

After reviewing the repressive measures that had been taken against the Church, Galen concluded he could no longer "quieten my conscience" with arguments for silence. Then, in July, the Nazi government seized hundreds of Catholic convents and monasteries, and levied a crushing 800,000-mark "war tax" on churches throughout the nation. Enraged, Galen took to the pulpit of his church in Münster; in three sermons that summer, he attacked the Nazi regime. In the first sermon, Galen singled out the Gestapo. "No single one of us is safe," he warned. "However guiltless he may know himself to be, he may still be taken from his home, deprived of his liberty and locked up in the cellars or concentration camps of the Gestapo."

Bishop von Galen's second sermon called on the members of his congregation to stand by their faith—while acknowledging that it was not easy to do. "Obedience to God and loyalty to conscience can cost you or me life, freedom or home," Galen said. "But it is better to die than to sin."

The mere fact that the bishop was using the pulpit to take issue with the state drew the attention of all Münster; his audiences grew larger each week. By the third sermon the church was packed to the doors as he delivered his strongest pronouncement yet—one that attacked the euthanasia program. He told his congregation that the Nazis were "putting to sleep" the patients in mental institutions all over Germany; he estimated the number of victims at 80,000 to 100,000. "The legal code of Germany still maintains that he who would murder another human being with premeditation should be punished by death," said Galen. He accused the government of killing "our poor sick humans, members of our own families, with premeditation," and with doing it at remote institutions, the better to keep the public from interfering. In almost every case, the bishop charged, some sort of illness was trumped up and the body was disposed of immediately to obscure the real cause of death. "This is murder!" he exclaimed.

Galen's words, coming as they did from a respected and temperate man of the cloth, had an electrifying effect on all Germany. The three sermons were read in other churches, both Catholic and Protestant. They were printed as leaflets and dropped into mailboxes all over the nation. They were picked up by foreign correspondents, then broadcast back to Germany over Allied airwaves.

In Berlin, Hitler and the other Nazi leaders were infuriated. Shortly after the third sermon Walter Tiessler, one of Goebbels' aides, prepared a memorandum for Hitler's secretary, Martin Bormann, suggesting that the offending bishop be hanged. Bormann doubtless found the proposal tempting, but he knew that to kill so public a figure as Galen would evoke a powerful reaction from the Vatican. Bormann also realized that the Nazis risked losing the support of German Catholics. Hitler concurred. He ordered that bishops and other high-ranking churchmen be left alone so "they have no opportunity to become martyrs." Bishop von Galen escaped punishment and continued to speak out from the pulpit.

Surprisingly, Bishop von Galen's sermons had succeeded in influencing Hitler; the ordinarily stubborn Führer quietly called off the euthanasia program. The leaflets conveying the churchman's words had an effect in another quarter as well. During the autumn of 1941, some of them landed in the mailbox of Robert Scholl, a tax consultant in the city of Ulm, about 300 miles southeast of Münster. Scholl and his wife Magdalene had a son and a daughter at the University of Munich; 22-year-old Hans was a medical student and Sophie, 20, was an undergraduate studying biology and philosophy. Thanks to Hans and Sophie, Galen's ideas were to generate a new phase of protest.

The Scholls seemed unlikely candidates for rebellion. Their Nazi credentials were impeccable; Hans had been a member of the Hitler Youth, and in 1936, when he was only 17, he had been rewarded for his zeal by being chosen to carry a flag at the annual Nuremberg rally. Sophie had been an equally loyal and enthusiastic member of the League of German Girls and had been made a group leader for her fervor. But both had been raised to think for themselves, and on emerging from their teens they began to bridle at Hitler's demand for "blind obedience and absolute discipline." At the university they found—independently of each other—that their irritation with the regime had turned into outright opposition. The catalyst that moved them to active dissent was a copy of Galen's sermon raging against the Nazi euthanasia program. According to the Scholls's older daughter, Inge, Hans read the leaflet and was elated. "Thank God," he cried, "someone has at last had the courage to speak out." He decided to add his own voice to the cause.

Acting without Sophie's knowledge, Hans purchased an old duplicating machine in Munich and enlisted the help of two like-minded friends, Christoph Probst and Alexander Schmorell. By May 1942 they were printing and distributing antigovernment leaflets signed "The White Rose," a name they chose because they liked its symbolic suggestion of purity. The first White Rose leaflet criticized the German people for being "spineless followers" of Hitler.

Sophie came upon the White Rose movement by accident. "My sister had hardly been in Munich six weeks," wrote Inge Scholl, who was still living at home in Ulm with her parents, "when something unbelievable happened at the university. Pamphlets were passed from hand to hand. They evoked a strange mixture of emotions among the students. Feelings of triumph and enthusiasm, rejection and anger surged and swelled." Sophie accepted one of the illegal leaflets and read its call for "passive resistance wherever you may be. Stop the course of this atheistic war machine before it is too late and the last of our youth have bled to death for the overweening pride of a subhuman. Do not forget that every nation gets the government it deserves."

Sophie went excitedly to Hans's room to tell him about the pamphlet. He was not there, so she decided to wait. While leafing through one of Hans's philosophy books, she discovered an underlined passage identical to one used in the leaflet she had just read. She realized that her brother might already be involved in the resistance movement, and when Hans returned she confronted him. "These days it is better not to know some things in case you endanger other people," he warned her. Sophie persisted until she got the truth—and then she persuaded Hans to let her join him in his work.

During the summer of 1942, the White Rose distributed three more leaflets. In them, the Scholls and a handful of friends called attention to the fate of Germany's Jews in the concentration camps and urged "sabotage in armament and war-industry plants, sabotage in gatherings, meetings, anything that promotes National Socialism."

By the following winter, the White Rose had broadened its efforts—members traveled by train to half a dozen cities in Germany and Austria to give their leaflets a wider readership. One night, emboldened by having continually eluded the Gestapo, the young protesters gleefully raced down the main streets of Munich painting the phrases "Down with Hitler!" and "Hitler is a mass murderer!" on walls at 70 different locations.

Then the violent reaction of their fellow students to Gauleiter Paul Giesler's speech in January of 1943 spurred the members of the White Rose to their most daring act. The furor over the student demonstration had hardly subsided when they decided to distribute their leaflets in broad daylight rather than scatter them under the cover of darkness as they had in the past. "Our nation has been shaken by the tragedy of Stalingrad, and 300,000 German men have been sacrificed," declared the latest leaflet. "Führer, we thank you!"

The leaflet ended with a call to action: "Our German name will always be in disgrace if we, the youth of Germany, do not rise and deal with our oppressors. Students, the eyes of the German people are upon us. They expect us to break the Nazi tyranny. The dead of Stalingrad demand it from us!"

Members of a student resistance group named the White Rose, Hans Scholl (left), his sister Sophie and a friend, Christoph Probst, confer in Munich in July of 1942. Hans's last words when all three went to the guillotine seven months later were "Long live freedom!"

On February 18, 1943, a sunny Thursday morning, the White Rose members began scattering leaflets throughout the lecture halls and corridors of the university; Hans and Sophie Scholl brazenly dropped some from atop a lecture hall. This time, however, they had pushed their luck too far. A university porter, who was a local party member, noted the blizzard of leaflets. He immediately locked the doors to the building and telephoned the police. Minutes later the Gestapo arrived and took the Scholls away to headquarters in Wittelsbach Palace, only a mile from the university. The Gestapo sent men to search Hans's room, looking for the names of others who might be involved. They found letters from Christoph Probst—who was now in Innsbruck—and arrested him, too.

After four days of unrelenting interrogation, the three students were brought to trial on February 22 before the People's Court, which tried only cases of treason and subversion, in Munich's Palace of Justice. The Nazis opened the trial to the public because they hoped to discourage further dissent by making an example of the Scholls and Probst. Presiding was Roland Freisler, who was known as the regime's "hanging judge" because he rarely showed defendants any mercy and seemed to find satisfaction in pronouncing the death sentence. Clad in a vivid scarlet robe, Freisler opened the trial by furiously sputtering out the charges against the three students to a courtroom that was crowded with soldiers, SS and SA men, and a few civilians: "Treason against the fatherland and preparation for high treason; calling for sabotage of war industry and subversion of the armed forces."

The defendants sat calmly as Freisler ranted. When he turned to them and demanded to know how any good German could do what the indictment alleged, Sophie answered for all three: "Somebody, after all, had to make a start. What we wrote and said is believed by many others. They just don't dare express themselves as we did."

As the trial proceeded through the morning, it became obvious that the verdict had been predetermined. Even so, the crowd was hushed as Freisler intoned, "For the protection of the German people in this time of mortal struggle there can be only one just verdict—the death penalty. With this sentence the People's Court demonstrates its solidarity with the fighting troops."

Robert and Magdalene Scholl arrived in the courtroom from their home at Ulm just in time to hear Freisler's verdict, which was to be carried out that very afternoon. They were allowed to see their condemned children briefly at Stadelheim Prison before the execution. Both young people seemed triumphantly happy. "This will create waves," Sophie told her mother. Before the afternoon was over, Hans, Christoph and Sophie were beheaded on the guillotine, an instrument the Nazis had brought back into use in 1933.

Without its leaders, the White Rose ceased its activities. Government retaliation did not end there, however. The Gestapo picked up 14 more people who had been associated with the group. Three were executed and the other 11 were given prison terms.

It is questionable whether the executions created the waves of protest that Sophie Scholl predicted. At its most effective, the White Rose had been only a thorn in the side of the Nazi colossus. Unlike Bishop von Galen, who had a wide following and the strength of the Church behind him, a few students were expendable. The Nazi state could and did exploit their fate in the press and on blood-red banners posted throughout the city of Munich in order to discourage further student disturbances. The publicity was hardly necessary. Anyone who opposed the regime was by then well aware that open dissent meant a quick death on the executioner's platform or a lingering one in the concentration camps.

"We never ceased wondering what more we could do," Inge Scholl was later to say. "We may seem, in retrospect, to have been ineffectual. But our real purpose, after all, was to let the truth be known, to tell the youth of Germany that it was being misused by the Nazis, and to give hope to the persecuted." In Nazi Germany, that in itself was heroic.

MOVIES TO SWAY THE NATION

A German magazine's montage of scenes from the movie Bomber Squadron Lützow features a bomber crew (center) and vignettes of Poland's "liberation."

A POTENT BLEND OF ART AND PROPAGANDA

In a cold and somber wartime Germany, less than a reichsmark bought an evening's escape to a snug chamber of illusion: the movie theater. So popular were Germany's 5,000 neighborhood theaters that in 1942 one billion tickets were sold—enough to send every German to the movies at least once a month. This prodigious moviegoing habit was encouraged by the top men in the Nazi regime.

On the orders of Minister of Propaganda Joseph Goebbels, theaters were warmer in winter than homes and were supplied with a variety of films picked for their popular appeal. But entertainment was not Goebbels' purpose; he saw the movie as a crucible for shaping the German mind.

To that end, Goebbels ran the state's movie industry with the ruthlessness of a Hollywood mogul, editing scripts and previewing—at times with Adolf Hitler at his side—every completed film. His objective was to produce a blend of art and propaganda "so profound and so vital that in the end the people fall under its spell and cannot escape from it."

A typical Goebbels-approved film played masterfully on a wide range of the viewer's emotions. A war thriller like *Bomber Squadron Lützow* simultaneously entertained with a boy-meets-girl romance, inspired patriotism through a heroic pilot's self-sacrifice, and spurred chauvinistic rage against Slavic "subhumans" who were shown holding ethnic Germans in thrall. A film entitled *Request Concert* portrayed selfless civilians and soldiers giving their all to win the War, inspired by the broadcasts of a popular weekly radio program. Historical dramas preached contempt for the enemy and invoked ancestral heroes in order to instill courage, discipline and faith in final victory.

In *Kolberg,* a lavish costume epic about a Prussian city's last-ditch resistance to Napoleon's armies, Goebbels hammered home the theme that, in his words, "a nation united at home and at the front can overcome any enemy." But in 1945 reality overtook illusion. A few weeks after the film's premiere in bomb-shattered Berlin, modern Kolberg fell to the Red Army, and on May 1 the Nazis' master imagemaker died by his own hand rather than surrender.

Hitler and Goebbels visit a set at the UFA movie studio, Germany's largest. Avid film fans, they monitored every aspect of German moviemaking.

Singer Marika Rökk belts out a ballad in the film *Request Concert*, a morale-raising smash hit that featured popular entertainers and fictional war heroes.

In the Nazi propaganda film *Uncle Kruger*, Transvaal President Paul Kruger, touring Buckingham Palace with a whisky-sodden Queen Victoria, makes a last bid for peace.

THE PRIZE-WINNING EPIC THAT TARNISHED BRITAIN

In *Uncle Kruger*, Nazi filmmakers sought to create an anti-British extravaganza that would equal Hollywood's *Gone with the Wind*, which moved Joseph Goebbels to jealous rage every time he saw it. *Uncle Kruger*, the tale of South African statesman Paul Kruger and his fight against the British, was produced by the actor Emil

Starving Boer women and girls await their meager rations behind the barbed-wire fence of an immense British concentration camp in South Africa. Other scenes from the film showed British soldiers indiscriminately bayoneting women and children.

Jannings, who also played the title role. With Goebbels' help, Jannings crafted a two-hour epic that won the foreign-film prize at the 1941 Venice Film Festival and was an instant sellout in Germany. The Nazi Security Service, which sent Goebbels reports of audience reactions to propaganda movies, called *Uncle Kruger* an "exceptional popular success." It was also effective propaganda. "The anti-British war mood," the agents gloated, "has been significantly increased and consolidated."

Captive Boer women confront a medical inspector and a brutish camp commandant with a can of rotten meat issued as rations. The officer rejects the evidence and shoots the woman who led the protest.

With rifles and Bibles, English missionaries in the film incite submissive black South African converts to attack Boer farmers. The Union Jack hangs over the altar of the thatched chapel.

In Homecoming, *a German maiden writhes in pain as a thuggish Pole wrenches the chain of a swastika medallion from her neck.*

RESCUING GERMANS FROM SLAVIC MASTERS

A primary target of the Nazis' most virulent film propaganda was the Slavic people, whom the Reich termed "subhuman." To help justify Hitler's invasions of Poland and Russia, the Propaganda Ministry commissioned a number of films glorifying the liberation of ethnic Germans, portrayed as suffering under Slavic despotism.

In *Bomber Squadron Lützow* a column of prisoners herded by Polish guards is miraculously delivered by strafing German warplanes that kill the guards and leave the German refugees unscathed.

In the 1941 film *Homecoming* there is a similar deliverance, but prolonged, so as to give the propagandists more breadth to depict Polish inhumanity and German suffering. *Homecoming* traces the growth of hostility toward Germans in Lodz, Poland. The German school is ransacked, a racist mob kills the heroine's fiancé in a theater, and then berserk villagers raze a farm and stone a girl to death.

When Hitler invades Poland, the Germans of Lodz are rounded up; awaiting death in a cellar, they comfort one another with visions of a day when "everything will be German." At the last minute, Luftwaffe planes drive off the guards and German tanks break down the prison walls.

In their secret hideout, German families huddle around a radio to hear Hitler proclaim their imminent liberation from Polish oppression. Later in the film they are discovered and herded off to a dungeon to await execution.

116

Standing ankle-deep in water, the imprisoned Germans of Lodz take comfort from the words of their blind patriarch, who proclaims that in Germany there is now "a voice that wakes up the whole world."

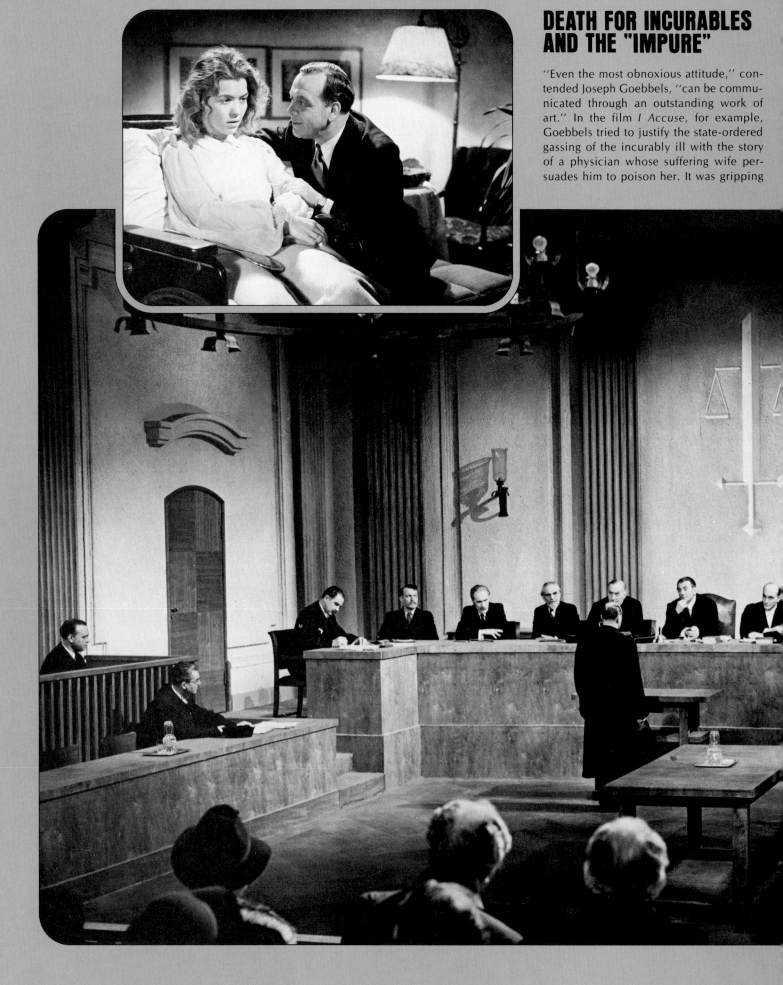

DEATH FOR INCURABLES AND THE "IMPURE"

"Even the most obnoxious attitude," contended Joseph Goebbels, "can be communicated through an outstanding work of art." In the film *I Accuse*, for example, Goebbels tried to justify the state-ordered gassing of the incurably ill with the story of a physician whose suffering wife persuades him to poison her. It was gripping courtroom drama, but no work of art, and it failed to silence the cries of outrage evoked by Hitler's euthanasia program.

A more pervasive theme in Nazi movies, that of racial purity, decreed "death before dishonor" for German women who were "defiled" by non-Aryans. To promote the Nazi ideal of pure womanhood and to emphasize the gulf between Aryans and "inferior" races, film scripts routinely killed off Aryan heroines who had been seduced by Jews or foreigners.

The heroine of The Jew Süss, actress Kristina Söderbaum, grimly submits to the rapacious villain of the title (top) to spare her imprisoned husband from torture. Then she drowns herself in the Neckar River, and her husband recovers her body (bottom). Typecast as a pure German maiden beset by alien suitors, the Swedish actress suffered so many last-reel drownings that she was dubbed "the national floating corpse."

"I love you," whispers the dying wife in I Accuse after her doctor-husband administers a lethal poison (inset). At left he accuses his judges of inhumanity for legally denying incurables a merciful release from pain. The movie's most convincing actors presented the arguments for mercy killing; less sympathetic characters took the opposing view.

Frederick the Great makes a Hitler-like speech to his officers, warning them that the Army must endure "terrible misfortunes" before achieving the decisive victory that "will change the face of Europe."

Extras costumed as Prussian infantrymen break into a charge in a lavish battle scene from The Great King, one of the Third Reich's most costly epics.

SHADES OF HITLER IN A WARRIOR-KING

The Great King premiered in March of 1942, not long after the Wehrmacht's first major setback in Russia. It reminded Germans that their forebears had once overcome greater reverses through the leadership and military genius of Frederick the Great, their revered 18th Century soldier-king. The movie's unsubtle message: What Prussians could do under Frederick, Germans could achieve behind Adolf Hitler.

Scenes carefully crafted to suggest comparisons with Hitler showed Frederick berating his defeatist generals after a disastrous battle, chastising and inspiring his men to greater discipline and fortitude, providentially escaping an assassination attempt, and vanquishing a host of foes.

Like the idealized Hitler of Goebbels' movie newsreels, the great king is portrayed as a lonely military genius, eating simple rations and going without sleep to plan the campaigns that will bring victory. When his men put their faith in him and follow orders unquestioningly, they win a series of spectacular battles and celebrate the successful end of the war with a Nazi-like parade in Berlin.

Crowds of moviegoers flocked to see the epic and were quick to catch its symbolism, which Goebbels hoped ''would toughen the German spirit of resistance that we need to triumph in this war.''

Propped against a captured enemy flag, a soldier dies on the battlefield at the feet of his king.

The Prussians' victory parade in Berlin symbolically promises Nazi triumph in World War II.

THE HEROIC EXAMPLE OF A CITY'S LAST STAND

The heroes of the Nazis' magnum opus, *Kolberg*, were historical figures: the besieged city's mayor, Nettelbeck, and the Prussian Army commander, General Gneisenau. Goebbels wrote much of the dialogue, pouring into the mayor's character his own diehard beliefs: "Better be buried under the ruins than capitulate!"

The movie, in color, was an extravaganza that took almost two years and 8.5 million marks to complete. To create the battle scenes, Goebbels supplied director Veit Harlan with 187,000 soldiers withheld at various times from the battlefronts; he also tied up defense industries with orders for 10,000 costumes, 100 railroad cars of salt to simulate snow, and vast quantities of blank ammunition. A "law of madness" prevailed, Harlan later wrote. "Hitler and Goebbels must have been obsessed by the idea that the film could be more useful than even a victory in Russia. They must have been hoping for a miracle."

No real-life miracle occurred. A few days before Goebbels committed suicide he and his staff met for a final showing of the film. He told them afterward: "In a hundred years they will show another fine color film describing the terrible days we are living through. Today you can choose the parts you will play then. Hold out now, so that the audience does not hoot and whistle when you appear on the screen."

General Gneisenau (left) persuades King Frederick William III to lead the people against Napoleon by recounting the defense of Kolberg. "From the ashes and the rubble," Gneisenau declares, "a new Reich will arise!"

In wartime Germany's last major film, extras in Napoleonic uniforms besiege the city of Kolberg. Not all the uniforms were authentic; soldiers in the rear ranks wore dyed Wehrmacht clothing with paper sashes.

Mayor Nettelbeck exhorts Kolberg's militia from a wagon seat. In the allegorical film he represented Nazi Party authority rallying the people to a last-ditch struggle.

Actors portraying townspeople, reassuringly unhurt despite constant bombardment, display the stoic endurance Goebbels expected of modern Germans in the last days of the Reich.

ONE FAMILY'S CHRONICLE

Friends and family of Karl (left) and Margarethe Kempowski (third from left) gather in 1943 on the day their daughter Ursula wed Ib Kai-Nielsen (both center).

YEARS OF FAITH AND SEPARATION

On a prewar holiday, Frau Kempowski and her young son Walter, who is happily munching on a rye wafer, visit a spa in the Harz Mountains.

The War crept up slowly on the Kempowski family of Rostock. In 1939 they were leading a comfortable, middle-class life, with a spacious apartment overlooking the port city on the Baltic, and a family shipping firm that had never been more profitable. Though the senior Kempowskis and their three children, like all Germans, faced nightly blackouts, food rationing and air-raid drills, they considered these annoyances merely temporary. The father, Karl, and the mother, Margarethe, scorned the Nazis, but their faith in the Army—and ultimate victory—was unshakable.

Indeed, Walter, the youngest, later remembered the first years of the War as a time of "sunny childhood" spent playing with his schoolmates, while his brother Robert devoted his time to friends who were addicted to American jazz. But in time the Kempowskis' carefree life changed; as the War edged closer it brought misfortune. The family firm's ocean-going freighter struck a British mine near the port of Wilhelmshaven and sank. Daughter Ursula's Danish fiancé, Ib Kai-Nielsen, was twice arrested by the Gestapo and held on suspicion of espionage. And in the spring of 1942 British bombers dropped nearly 1,000 tons of bombs on Rostock, leaving much of the city in ruins.

Though the close-knit clan managed to elude disaster, events conspired to separate them. Both Karl and his son Robert were drafted. Ursula was conscripted for the National Labor Service; when her stint was over, she married Ib and moved to Lübeck. "We are a tiny family now, aren't we?" Margarethe Kempowski said sadly to Walter, her last child at home. In the last months of the War, even the consolation of Walter's company was taken from her when the Wehrmacht drafted the 15-year-old as a courier.

Walter returned to Rostock in late April, 1945, only a few days ahead of the advancing Red Army. He urged his mother to join the thousands of refugees fleeing westward to the relative safety of the British and American lines, but she refused to abandon her home. "When peace comes," she said, "they'll be needing people here." So they stayed to face the uncertainties of Soviet occupation together.

Storm Troopers parade in Rostock after Hitler took power. Frau Kempowski asked her husband, "Who are those men in brown—garbage collectors?"

The Kempowskis' apartment (below) occupied three stories over a street-level bookshop. Margarethe grew cacti and geraniums on the rear balcony (right), adding a splash of color to the urban neighborhood.

Ursula models her Labor Service work uniform.

A HOME KEPT GOING BY A RESOLUTE MOTHER

For a time after her husband was drafted and her daughter left for service with the National Labor Corps, Margarethe Kempowski cared for her home and her sons alone—no easy task in wartime.

During the 1942 air raid on Rostock she raced repeatedly from the cellar shelter to the attic to put out fires that had started there. "Mother must have run upstairs a hundred times, despite the bombs," Walter later boasted to his father.

When future son-in-law Ib was arrested on suspicion of providing maps of the city to the British, Frau Kempowski marched over to police headquarters to defend him. "He's a harmless boy. I'd let him go," she told a Gestapo agent. Upon his release, Ib moved in with the Kempowskis because his own home had been bombed out. "Not all Germans are bad," Frau Kempowski told the angry young Dane. "Nazis and Germans aren't the same."

A serene Frau Kempowski awaits guests at home.

Ursula smiles with Ib, who worked for her father.

Friends commiserate after the 1942 raid on Rostock. "Four high-explosive and 50 incendiary bombs fell on our street in one night," Walter recalled.

A MATURITY HASTENED BY WAR

Walter Kempowski was only 10 years old when the War began, his life untroubled except for academic problems with Latin and math. His days were filled with school and play, his evenings with books of science fiction and adventure, which he read with a flashlight after bedtime.

Everyone's childhood in wartime Germany, however, was colored by Nazism. As a member of the Hitler Youth, Walter participated in twice-weekly indoctrination meetings, song fests and hikes. He and his friends played war with Nazi toys: Storm Troopers, and small Führers with movable arms for the "*Sieg Heil!*" salute.

As he grew older, Walter began to rebel against the Hitler Youth. The increasing drills and harassment from young toughs in the organization were more than he could stand. By the age of 14, he was skipping most of the meetings and had stopped wearing his uniform.

Walter (top row, second from right) and his chums gather in 1941 outside their school. It was destroyed by bombs a year later.

A party organized for children during a holiday at the spa in Alexisbad gives Walter a chance to parade his talents as a marshal.

A fire hose snakes up the stairs of the bombed-out ruins of Walter's school. The children returned when the fires died, and salvaged their teacher's grade book as a memento.

Walter sports the Hitler Youth winter uniform that he wore to meetings, on hiking trips and on his group's good-will missions.

Night Fighters Meet the Enemy, one of Walter Kempowski's favorite books, imaginatively described the awful fate that awaited Allied bomber crews over Germany.

Walter (foreground) and two friends, bundled in their Hitler Youth uniforms, haul a sled loaded with coal for elderly people who are unable to fetch their own rations.

FATHER AND SON SERVING THE REICH

Karl Kempowski, a veteran of World War I, volunteered for active duty in 1939 but was rejected because he had once belonged to the Freemasons, an international organization that the Nazis distrusted. He kept busy with his shipping firm until his freighter, the *Consul Hintz*, was sunk by a mine. Before the vessel could be replaced, the Wehrmacht drafted Kempowski and assigned him as an officer on ammunition trains in the West. He was later transferred to the town of Garz in Pomerania to oversee POWs.

The Kempowskis' son Robert was also exempted from military service at first because of poor eyesight. Robert was a slight, mildly rebellious youth whom his strict but loving father chastised for his long locks "like a hairdresser's" and for his devotion to jazz. Robert was the last of his crowd to be drafted.

As he left for war he worried about his precious phonograph records; it would be all right for Walter to play them, he said, then added sternly: "But remember to change the needle often."

The Kempowskis' 30-year-old, 2,500-ton ship, the Consul Hintz (above), was used to transport a variety of cargo. The ship was sunk in 1940, and was replaced a year later by a Latvian freighter that the Germans had confiscated.

Army Captain Karl Kempowski (left) wraps an arm around his friend and fellow officer, Captain Hermann Müller, in an informal interlude during an assignment in Poland.

Robert Kempowski (far left) assumes a jaunty stance with fellow members of his circle, who were enthusiastic devotees of American jazz. All the youths were drafted; only Robert and Gerhard West (fourth from left) survived the War.

Robert "jazzes it up"—his brother's phrase—on the balcony of the Kempowski family apartment. As the War progressed, jazz recordings grew scarce; in Rostock they could be found only on the back shelves of the last record store left standing.

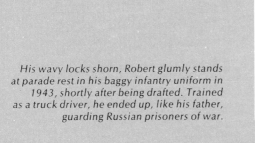

His wavy locks shorn, Robert glumly stands at parade rest in his baggy infantry uniform in 1943, shortly after being drafted. Trained as a truck driver, he ended up, like his father, guarding Russian prisoners of war.

A NARROW ESCAPE, A REUNION DELAYED

In late February, 1945, Ib and Ursula received a letter from Frau Kempowski that said: "I've had no news of your father. Robert is still in Kolberg, and Walter has been called up. It is quiet and dead without him, and I miss my children terribly."

Assigned to courier duty, Walter was in Berlin on a mission in late April when he heard the news one morning that Russian troops had surrounded the city. He hurried north toward Rostock, nearly overcome by the "smell of mortar, burning paper and corpses." As he neared Oranienburg, the boy learned that the Russians had outpaced him; he was forced to turn south and then west through Spandau to find an opening in the Soviet lines. After walking for hours through Russian-held territory, Walter was finally able to hitch a ride on a milk truck to a depot, where he caught a refugee-packed train home.

Walter and his mother watched the Soviets take over the city, but the ensuing peace brought little relief to the Kempowskis. Karl was still missing. A year of dread elapsed before the family learned that, just before the War ended, he had been killed in a Russian air raid while trying to escape from East Prussia by sea.

Another ordeal commenced. In 1948 Margarethe and her two sons were imprisoned by Soviet authorities on trumped-up charges of passing industrial secrets to the Americans. Robert and Walter each served eight years at hard labor; their mother was released after six years in prison. Not until 1956 (opposite) was the Kempowski family reunited.

In the winter of 1945, Walter Kempowski pauses before leaving his barracks on a courier mission. His white scarf violated dress-code regulations, but he wore it anyway because he considered it dashing.

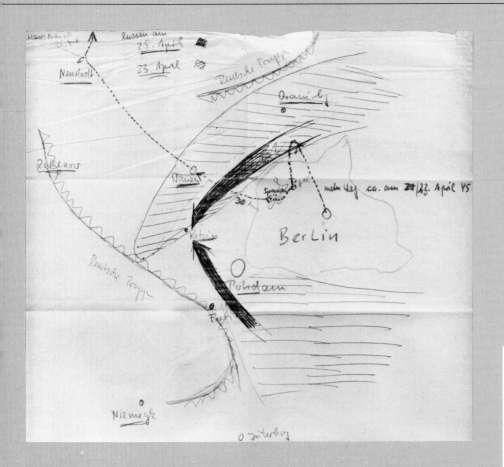

A map drawn by Walter describes his escape from Berlin. The striped areas indicate the Red Army advance against German troops (wavy lines) as of April 23, 1945, and the two black arrows show the Soviets' pincers movement on Ketzin, completed on April 25. The dotted line traces Walter's precarious flight through Russian lines.

The family smiles for a group portrait at their first postwar reunion, which was dominated by remembrances of Karl Kempowski (inset). "One question will always torment me," Walter said of his father. "Why should a 42-year-old man fight for the Nazis, whom he couldn't stand?"

4

On the evening of Saturday, May 30, 1942, Captain Erich Behnke of the Cologne Fire Department sat outside the firehouse playing cards with some of his comrades. It was an unusually lovely evening, and many other citizens of Cologne were outside enjoying it. Some strolled the embankments along the Rhine River, others sat at sidewalk cafés drinking the local white wine. The parks, particularly the Stadtwald, were just emptying of the crowds that had come to town to shop or watch the morning horse race at Riehl, on the edge of the city. Off-duty soldiers walked the narrow streets of the red-light district between the railroad station and the river.

The city's mood was good in this third year of the War. There had been no air-raid alarm in two months. It was rumored there was to be an increase in food rations, particularly of fruit and vegetables. The Nazi leadership had promised that this summer's offensive on the Eastern Front would finally defeat the Russians and lead to the peace that had begun to seem so elusive.

Many years afterward, men and women would remember with unusual clarity what they were doing on that calm spring evening. Richard Frank, a bank employee, was bowling with a group of friends, and ran up what was for him a particularly good score. Hans Sion, owner of one of Cologne's famous breweries, was drinking beer with a few favored customers in a beer hall that he owned. Hildegarde Steinborn, 30 years old and four months pregnant, was listening to the popular singer Lala Andersen on the radio. Dr. Berta Weigand-Fellinger, off duty after a hard day at Eduardis Hospital, was taking care of her twin sister's children while the sister was away. Also staying in the house was a family friend, a Wehrmacht lieutenant by the name of Sobeck. The children were chattering about the film they had seen that afternoon starring the celebrated comedian Heinz Ruhmann.

Most of Cologne was in bed by 11 p.m., with a full moon shining on the Rhine. At precisely 11:45 the air-raid sirens began to shrill.

Dr. Weigand-Fellinger awoke immediately, but at first she was not worried: She thought it would be another light raid of the kind the city had experienced before. Then the earth started to tremble and shake, and Lieutenant Sobeck burst into her room. "Out!" he shouted. "Out! The gas

THE CONFLICT COMES HOME

mains have been hit! We'll burn alive!" They ran to an air-raid shelter through streets that were already ablaze.

Hildegarde Steinborn was halfway down the steps into a cellar shelter when "what seemed like a ghostly hand picked me up and threw me into the air. Everyone in the cellar clung to one another, as the walls appeared to fall on us. Plaster rained down on our upturned faces; shrapnel whizzed through the air. The light went out suddenly. The door was ripped off by a blast and now outside we could see the flames tearing upward everywhere."

Hans Sion made it to the bunker beneath Cologne Cathedral, but he was blinded for days after running through an "inferno of swirling phosphorus and clouds of smoke." Richard Frank, who had lingered over his bowling, was crossing a river bridge when the sirens sounded. He ran to the nearest air-raid shelter, but it had already been locked. In desperation, he doubled back and hid under the bridge with some soldiers. "We huddled together in this hail of bombs," he recalled, "watching with horror the reflection of the burning city in the waters of the river." A bomb fragment tore off a young soldier's leg, and Frank remembered that for an hour the man lay moaning "while the inferno above and around us seemed to continue forever."

Fire Captain Behnke rushed to the inner city, to find buildings and trees ablaze, with "phosphorus sticking to their trunks and branches." In the narrow streets he saw corpses clinging to the iron bars of basement windows, suffocated by fires that had sucked the oxygen from the air. Survivors emerged to "stare into the flames, blinded. Again and again I heard them cry 'We can't see! Where are we?' "

With his wife and small daughter, journalist Josef Fischer hurried to the shelter of their building. The sensation he experienced there was like nothing he had felt before: "Heavy air pressure surges into the room, affects the lungs and eardrums. I open and close my mouth. Nothing helps. The knees begin to weaken, the body becomes light, and suddenly a sucking sensation follows the pressure. What was agonizing pressure before becomes total emptiness. And again: pressure, suction, pressure, suction." His terrified wife asked him to hold their child: "We huddle together like animals during a violent thunderstorm."

The attack lasted 90 minutes, leaving Cologne a raging inferno. An unprecedented 1,080 bombers had dropped 2,000 tons of explosives in the greatest single air attack thus far in the War. All told, fewer than 500 people died in the raid, and 5,000 were injured. Some 600 acres of the city were devastated, however, and 45,000 people were left homeless. For days the roads leading from the stricken city were clogged with refugees.

After that night of horror, the German home front was never again the same. Cologne marked the beginning of a new and terrible kind of warfare that would kill 500,000 civilians, displace uncounted millions, and test the mettle of the German people as it had never been tested before. Although there had been earlier incendiary raids—most notably the 234-plane attack on Lübeck and the 100-plane attack on the Baltic port of Rostock in the early spring of 1942—nothing on the scale of the Cologne raid had been even imagined. When Winston Churchill called it a herald of what Germany would receive in the future, he was sounding not only the hopes of the English but the worst fears of the Germans. Within days, Cologne became "the focal point of discussions everywhere," according to a secret SD report of June 4, 1942. What the populace feared, noted the report, was that such attacks would "continue with the same intensity and be spread to other towns."

Publicly, the Nazi Party minimized the importance of the Cologne raid, but privately most of the leadership understood full well what it meant for the urban population. Hermann Göring refused to believe the statistics of the raid. "It's impossible!" he declared. "That many bombs cannot be dropped in a single night!" But his attitude was not shared by the more pragmatic Joseph Goebbels, who hastened to Cologne to see for himself. He came away badly shaken. "The effects of bomb warfare are horrible when one looks at individual cases," he wrote in his diary. Goebbels consoled himself that once the Luftwaffe had recovered from losses suffered on the Russian front, it would make night bombing so costly for the English that another 1,000-bomber raid would be impossible. Until that time, he wrote, civilians must simply put up with life under the bombs.

In the months following Cologne, German civilians did just that—and with amazing resilience and courage. The rhythm of life in the bombing zones was now dictated by a small gadget called a *Drahtfunk* (literally, "cable radio") that was attached to standard radios. Kept going day and night, it emitted a monotonous *tock-tock* sound when no enemy bombers were over the Reich, but changed to an insistent *ping-ping* whenever bombers crossed the frontier. Then at regular intervals an announcer would give the exact position, number and type of enemy aircraft heading for a specific target.

Although sirens and air-raid wardens warned of impending attacks, many people preferred not to rely on them; instead, families and neighbors divided the night into watches of *"Drahtfunk* duty,*"* taking turns sitting by the radio on alert for the *ping-ping* to start. The radio became so much a part of her family's life, one housewife recalled, that her three-year-old niece took the warnings as a game; every time the pinging sound came on she scrambled under the table with her coat and handbag, calling "Achtung! East course, taking east course!"

Many city dwellers slept in all-purpose outfits so they could jump out of bed and race to the shelters without pausing to dress. With films, concerts and other public events now forced to close by 7 o'clock, people ate early and went to bed shortly after dark. The more foresighted cooked food in advance while the gas and electricity were still on, then placed the food under mattresses in towel-wrapped containers to keep it warm. Bathtubs and pans were kept filled with water in case the water mains were struck by bombs. Families whose homes had yards hoarded sticks and bits of wood so that they could cook over open fires if they had to.

In ways that surprised even themselves, people learned to improvise and to cope. When cotton thread disappeared from the market, women started darning clothes with string dyed with shoe polish. Men stropped old razor blades into a semblance of sharpness by running them round and round the inside of a glass jar. When dry-cleaning establishments closed down for lack of personnel, people learned to press garments by soaping them along the desired crease, placing them beneath a mattress and sleeping on them. Because hats were a hindrance in air-raid shelters, women started wearing turbans instead.

At about the time of the Cologne raid—contrary to the optimistic rumor—new reductions in meat, lard and butter rations were announced. Not all regions were affected equally. People in the bombing zones automatically received more generous allocations as part of the government's effort to stiffen morale. Farmers were designated "self-suppliers," and they were excluded from the rationing scheme; although there were strict limitations on the amount of produce the farmers could keep for themselves, most of them managed to grow considerably more than they declared, and they continued to eat as well as they had before the War.

For those with no access to farm produce, the quality of the daily diet declined sharply in the summer of 1942. Bread by then contained so many admixtures that it was extremely hard to digest. A common box lunch for workers consisted of sandwiches spread with yeast, flour, a little fat or margarine, and a few specks of sausage or spices for flavor. The film actress Hildegarde Neff, who grew up in wartime Berlin, recalled that her staple diet was composed largely of thin, ersatz coffee, margarine on rolls made with water rather than milk, and "powdered eggs diluted and stirred, scrambled and fried, tasting of glue."

New clothing, when it was available at all, had declined in quality. There was a special bristly feel to wartime wool, Hildegarde Neff recalled, because it came from ill-cared-for sheep that were never curried. As clothes wore out, it became almost impossible to have them repaired. Only a few

On leave from the Russian front, a soldier chalks a message on the wall of his bombed-out home in Hamburg, asking for news of his wife following a week of devastating air raids in the summer of 1943. After major Allied raids, German commanders sometimes granted soldiers up to 20 days' furlough to search for and assist their families.

tailors remained in business, and shoemakers were so deluged with repair jobs that they kept their doors locked for all but a few hours a week. Noting the public's frustration, the Nazi Party newspaper *Das Schwarze Korps* in July 1942 scolded those who got upset over a few torn garments, which it said were a small price for final victory.

That summer the government commissioned surveys to determine what consumer goods people needed most urgently. High on the list were tools for home repair of all sorts, together with household implements such as sieves, cooking pots, Thermos bottles, and pails for combating air-raid fires. Also in short supply were scissors, pocket knives, shoelaces and even string. In some cities there was not a flashlight to be found, although they were indispensable for moving through the blacked-out streets.

Unable to promise any increase in consumer goods, government propagandists tried to encourage ingenuity in using what little was available. One proposal was that housewives form "community kitchens" and pool their utensils by passing them from family to family according to a prearranged schedule. With too much money in circulation and too few goods, most people eventually fell back on a barter system as the only possible way to obtain what they needed. A piece of furniture ceased to be a consumer commodity and became an item of exchange. Newspapers were full of advertisements in which people offered to swap a radio for a bicycle, an umbrella for a kitchen pot or a garbage pail for a woolen blanket.

The government attempted to maintain a modicum of control over the barter market by defining which transactions were lawful and which were not. In general it was forbidden to barter anything controlled by rationing. Nevertheless, illegal exchanges flourished. People lucky enough to have surplus rationed goods engaged in what became known as "stoop transactions"—so called from the stealthy stooping posture shopkeepers assumed as they unearthed some unobtainable piece of merchandise from beneath a counter to trade for an equally rare rationed commodity handed over by the customer.

For two months in the summer of 1942 the government tried to stamp out the stoop transactions by staging widely publicized trials of citizens accused of illicit trading. Several dozen people were sentenced to death, among them Otto and Martha Schnellert of Erfurt, who were said to have exchanged worn articles of clothing for rationed food. But security-service reports suggested that the proceedings did little good and may instead have done some harm, for they drew public attention to the fact that important Nazis, who benefited the most from black-market transactions, were never brought to trial.

For those who had influence or goods to barter, virtually anything was still obtainable in the cities. Fashionable restaurants that catered to high officials in government and industry were especially favored. They could procure items such as game, fish and fowl that most citizens had not seen for a year or more. One of the most popular spots in Berlin was the restaurant in the Hotel Adlon; the restaurant required no ration coupons for good food and wines, and beneath the hotel there was a supposedly bombproof shelter with a concrete roof 30 feet thick. On a typical evening, recalled journalist Ursula von Kardorff, the Adlon attracted a crowd "straight out of a novelette." In addition to "party big shots in snappy uniforms," there were "German and foreign diplomats, actors, fashionable suburban housewives, businessmen with pigskin briefcases reeking of 'armaments' and loose women of every kind."

Those who got tables at the Adlon by buying their way into the manager's favor, said Kardorff, "had to run the gantlet of envious glances" as they walked from the bar through the lobby to the dining room. But once they were seated, they could relax: "Even when darkness begins to fall no one here looks anxiously around or strains his ears to catch the sound of the alert. Here one is safe and can sip one's red wine in peace before going down, leather suitcase in hand, to take refuge from the bombs."

The War produced a new wealthy class. Predictably, the munitions makers profited, but so did a whole range of party functionaries, together with people oddly favored by the inflated wartime economy. A Berlin wine waiter bought himself a house in the country from tips he received in cash and commodities. Butchers were suddenly wealthier than many of their favored clients.

Because savings seemed pointless, people spent recklessly. Soldiers home from the front handed out tips amounting to two weeks' pay. At the race track at Hoppegarten outside

Berlin, people stood in line at the betting windows as long as they had anything in their pockets. When a cleaning woman in Berlin got bombed out and was given emergency clothing coupons, she surprised her employer by purchasing her new clothes at the smartest couturier left in the city.

Party newspapers complained that people wanted only to amuse themselves or to hunt for commodities, and that they had lost all interest in the progress of the War. Noting a new surliness in the public mood, Goebbels proclaimed Politeness Weeks, during which people were supposed to work together more amicably and stop their incessant grumbling. But the real problem, according to an unpublished government report in the autumn of 1942, was that people were becoming weary. Their mood, said the report, could be summed up in a remark that was heard with variations over and over: "Who would have thought, after the great victories at the beginning, that the War would take this course and drag on so long?"

By the last weeks of 1942, opinion research showed that although most people still believed Germany would win the War, there was growing uneasiness caused by the Allied landings in North Africa and by the rout of Field Marshal Erwin Rommel's army at El Alamein. In addition, the summer offensive in the East had not produced the decisive results the public expected. Instead, the Russian armies seemed stronger than ever.

Then, early in 1943, came the disaster to German arms at Stalingrad. News of the Sixth Army's surrender jolted people into the realization for the first time that Germany might well lose the War. It also shook their faith in Hitler. A Reich Chancellery report warned that "people now even dare to criticize the person of the Führer openly and attack him in a hateful and spiteful way." Else Wendel of Berlin recalled the shock she felt upon visiting an old friend who had lost her husband at Stalingrad: "I found, as she opened the door, a thin old woman in black, not the proud, confident woman I had known." The mourning woman said that what haunted her was a rumor that the Sixth Army could have escaped encirclement at Stalingrad but that Hitler had forbidden it. "I was frightened," Else Wendel remembered. "No, impos-

sible," I said. "It would be plain murder. Hitler would never do such a thing." Very slowly the widow lifted her head. "I am not so sure," she said.

After Stalingrad, recalled production czar Albert Speer, even Goebbels had begun "to doubt in Hitler's star and thus in victory—and so had we." But Goebbels kept his doubts to himself, and in fact launched a new propaganda offensive to invigorate the home front. On the 18th of February, he delivered an emotional speech at Berlin's Sports Palace. To ensure a rousing response, he had thousands of faithful party members brought in from all across the country. Loudspeakers were positioned around the vast auditorium to broadcast recorded applause.

At the height of his appeal, Goebbels asked the audience 10 questions of mounting intensity: Did they believe in final victory, were they willing to endure all hardships, would they endorse the death penalty for shirkers? The key question came last: "Do you want Total War?" In unison, the well-drilled audience roared "Yes!" Flag-waving demonstrations erupted, and once more the Sports Palace echoed with the familiar cries of "Hail, the Führer!" and "Leader, command, we follow!" A German writer present said people were worked into such a frenzy that had Goebbels asked them if they were prepared to die, they all would have shouted "Yes!"

Goebbels used the "mandate" given him by the response to his Total War speech to tighten the screws on the home front. It was ridiculous, he said, to have more than six million workers still turning out consumer products, 1.5 million German women still toiling as maids and cooks, and 100,000 restaurants and amusement centers still functioning almost as they had in 1939. Declaring his resolve to "act quickly and recklessly" to put the country on a war footing, he ordered that all conceivable sources of manpower be tapped, including those that had been passed over during an earlier "total" mobilization in January 1942.

Criminals serving time in state prisons now found themselves mobilized. Vast sheds were erected in the prison yards and filled with every kind of equipment, from looms for making cloth to iron forges to giant steel presses. One prison in southern Germany not only manufactured 3,000 garments and 10,000 pairs of wooden shoes a month but

took in tattered clothing, which most people had been reduced to wearing by the fourth winter of the War, and patched it up for another few months' wear.

Hitler Youth leader Arthur Axmann announced that he would provide six million children for industry and agriculture by recruiting those in the age group 10 to 15. The younger ones were assigned to help farmers with the harvest and to collect old rags, clothing and scrap for the war industries. The older ones became so-called flak helpers—part-time antiaircraft gunners—and performed heavy (and often dangerous) work on merchant ships.

All men aged 16 to 65 and all women aged 17 to 50 had to register for compulsory labor allocation. Up to this point in the War, Hitler had consistently opposed compulsory labor for women on the ground that their place was at home producing and raising babies. But now the shock of Stalingrad made him reluctantly change his mind. Goebbels pledged that he would "see to it that even the daughters of plutocrats cannot shirk this obligation."

Elderly men living on pensions were urged to go back to work in factories or on farms. The newspapers made much of a photograph of an 81-year-old man busy in a brewery cellar repairing damaged beer kegs with a hammer. People already fully employed were told to do more or to use their time better. Food Minister Herbert Backe declared that "the country woman must add a few hours to her daily work of 14 to 16 hours." Hairdressers were permitted only to cut hair and give shampoos, not to waste their time with permanent waves. People were forbidden to pursue celebrities for their autographs on the ground that the time might be better spent in work that would benefit the nation. Some communities introduced time-saving ordinances so nonsensical that they were ridiculed in the press—including prohibitions against card-playing in cafés and against taking the family dog out for a walk.

Many small businesses and shops were closed down so that their personnel could be assigned to essential war industries. The manufacture of a great number of consumer goods—among them cosmetics, fountain pens, toys and photographic materials for civilian use—was prohibited. Stricter penalties were established for infractions in the workplace, and the resulting trials were widely publicized. Offenses against plant discipline brought two years in pris-

German workers harvest poppies on the lawn of Französischer Cathedral in the center of Berlin. The poppies were in demand as the base element in the painkiller morphine and as a source of cooking oil. Urban gardens also supplied the home front with cabbage, mustard and herbs.

on; simple tardiness was punished with sentences of two to three months.

Yet this second Total Mobilization was a disappointment to Goebbels and to other party leaders. The introduction of compulsory labor yielded no more than 1.3 million full-time workers to replace those summoned to the Army to make up losses on the Eastern Front. Women in particular showed little enthusiasm for war work; many of them managed to avoid it by getting pregnant and thus obtaining an automatic exemption. In the relatively comfortable middle class, there were many cases of fathers and husbands claiming their daughters and wives as secretaries to prevent their assignment to factories.

In party circles, the response was no better. Hitler's secretary, Martin Bormann, categorically refused to allow any party workers, male or female, to be included in the new mobilization. Joseph Goebbels learned the limits of his colleagues' patriotism when his wife dismissed the family cook so that she could work in a munitions factory—only to find that she had been promptly hired by another Nazi official. Observing the unruly mobilization of the home front, soldiers newly returned from Russia were reported as saying: "The Russians are conducting Total War, we are fighting an elegant war."

The bulk of the 1.3 million new workers came from the occupied territories. Although German industry had begun forcibly recruiting foreign workers as early as 1941, the real influx did not start until the setbacks in the East during the winter of 1942. By the spring of 1943 there were 12 million foreign workers in Germany, including prisoners of war. They amounted to 40 per cent of the nation's work force, and in some arms factories 90 per cent of the workers were non-German.

Although many Germans never came in contact with them, impressed laborers constituted an entire alien society within the Reich. Ursula von Kardorff recalled the astonishment she felt one day in downtown Berlin when she heard the air-raid sirens and raced into the nearest shelter: "It was all rather as I imagine Shanghai to be," she wrote. "Ragged, romantic-looking characters in padded jackets, with high, Slavic cheekbones, mixed with fair-haired Danes and Norwegians, smartly turned-out Frenchwomen, Poles casting looks of hatred at everybody, fragile, chilly Italians—a

mingling of races such as can never before have been seen in any German city. The people down there are almost all foreigners and one hears hardly a word of German spoken. Most of them are conscripted workers in the armaments factories."

The alien workers had their own canteens, in which they put on stage shows, and they even published their own newspapers. The government set up "foreigner" brothels for them in most large towns. By 1943 there were 60 such establishments employing 600 prostitutes. Unfortunately, the foreigners did not always play by the rules: A secret-service report of 1943 recounted that a group of Hamburg prostitutes with "no sense of propriety" were observed taking foreign workers up to rooms that had "always been recognized as reserved for loyal German workers and for soldiers up to and including the rank of sergeant."

Part of the government's solicitude for the foreigners' entertainment was prompted by a fear that they would "pollute" German womanhood if left to their own devices. Court records indicate that in the absence of German men, many women did indeed have relations with foreigners. When such cases were reported, the foreign worker was put to death and the woman was thrown in jail for "racial

shame.'' Thus two married women in Gera were imprisoned for having intercourse with a French prisoner of war working for a German farmer, and an anonymous ''M'' in Bayreuth went to jail for her love affair with a Polish man. In spite of the severe penalties, incidents of racial shame became so prevalent that the secret service felt compelled to issue a report on the subject, entitled ''The Immoral Behavior of German Women.''

The sheer number of non-Germans in the Reich made the leadership uneasy. Often the foreigners were likened to a kind of Trojan horse within the walls of the state, capable of toppling the regime if they should ever revolt. In the factories, SS troops stood constant guard over them with automatic pistols. When Allied bombers passed overhead, the factory gates often were locked and machine guns were trained on the entrance. A few carefully selected foreigners were recruited as Gestapo spies to report on the activities and conversation of the workers when they were away from the factories.

A Gestapo report of 1943 emphasized the particular hatred of Germans felt by the *Ostarbeiter,* workers from the East whose supposed racial inferiority made them special targets of Nazi brutality. According to the report, the *Ostarbeiter* spoke frequently of sabotaging German industry and of torturing individual Germans after the Russian victory. When a propaganda leaflet with a picture of the Führer on the front was circulated in factories, the alien workers were said to have stabbed out the picture's eyes with pins and needles. A female worker was quoted as writing in a censored letter that she had been brought to Germany by train, but that after the War German women would have to march to Siberia on foot. Another correspondent was reported to have shown obvious delight in describing the horror of the air raids and the numbers of dead Germans she had seen littering the streets.

Party leaders in many areas of Germany organized local militia units as protection against revolt and as a means of tying the populace more closely to the regime. Professors at the University of Bonn, for example, were instructed in shooting and were taught to fear the workers as a subversive force that might any day explode.

In the spring of 1943, most Germans were less worried about the foreign workers than they were about the growing fleets of Allied bombers roaring over their cities. After the Cologne raid there had been a lull because in 1942 the British lacked the planes to sustain attacks of such magnitude. In addition, the RAF's navigational aids were inadequate for truly accurate night bombing. But by the end of the year the British had developed excellent position-finding radar. At the same time, the American Eighth Air Force was rapidly building up its operational strength to parity with RAF Bomber Command.

In contrast to the British, the Americans favored a daylight bombing strategy—partly because they had great expectations for their new Norden bombsight and partly because they were confident that the American B-17 Flying Fortresses and B-24 Liberators could fight off Luftwaffe daylight attacks better than the British bombers could. By the late winter of 1943 the two Allied air forces were strong enough to launch a joint round-the-clock offensive of daytime and nighttime bombing that gradually blanketed all of urban

Under armed surveillance by a German guard, French miners move a coal car onto a train in the Artois region of France. By 1943 an estimated seven million workers were laboring for Germany in occupied lands.

Soviet forced laborers collapse during a rest break at a mine in eastern Germany. Polish and Russian ''East workers'' wore convicts' uniforms and worked 14-hour days at the most physically demanding jobs. They received a salary that just covered the inflated prices they were charged for room, board and clothing.

143

Germany. Not until it had wreaked destruction on virtually every city of more than 100,000 inhabitants did the campaign come to an end.

For those in the path of the terror, a new way of life began. Instead of waiting for the *Drahtfunk* warning to sound, many citizens now began lining up at the public shelters as soon as it got dark so they would be assured of getting a place. The mood in the shelters ranged from stoic to frivolous to hysterical. In Berlin, Else Wendel looked at the faces of the people around her and was reminded of "a vast crowd watching a funeral." Hildegarde Neff, on the other hand, recalled soldiers passing the evening by "sliding the length of the bunker on their hobnailed boots like children on a frozen pond." In Augsburg, Ursula von Kardorff sat opposite some Hitler Youth officials and their girl friends: "At first they were noisy and insolent, then, as things got worse, they knelt in a circle on the floor, clutched at one another and ducked every time there was a heavy explosion. In the end they were praying."

Living, eating, sleeping, loving and sometimes dying underground, people developed the same ties of loyalty to their shelter communities that in peacetime they had felt for their cities and neighborhoods. Erich Kuby of Berlin recalled that the regulars with whom he huddled almost nightly were suspicious of the people in other shelters and were convinced that their own was the safest in Berlin. Many young people were unshakably loyal to the Berlin Zoo shelter because the spiral stone staircase leading into it had convenient niches where couples could embrace as the bombs fell.

Shelter dwellers became experts in survival. They learned to keep their mouths open to protect their eardrums from concussion and to practice shallow breathing when the ventilators had to be closed because of fires raging outside. When the heat became too intense and the explosions dangerously close, people wrapped themselves in wet sheets, donned steel helmets and covered their eyes with gauze to guard against being blinded in the event of a direct hit on the shelter by high-explosive and phosphorus bombs. Christabel Bielenberg experienced one particularly heavy raid on Berlin that rocked her entire shelter. She was surprised to hear a small, elderly woman next to her firmly

counting aloud over the crash of the bombs. She stopped at the number eight and lowered her legs, which had been propped against an abutment of the wall opposite. "An American carpet raid," the woman explained, referring to the practice of carpeting a target with bombs laid down in a grid pattern. She added with professional exactitude: "Eight bombs in each bomb cradle; peace now until the next wave comes over."

Everybody came to recognize the characteristic sounds of different bombs. The most dangerous was a piercing whistle, which meant that a high explosive was descending almost directly on the shelter. But the sound most feared was a kind of gurgle, followed by a buzzing. "I heard this awful noise," recalled Christina Knauth, an American girl interned with her mother and her sisters, Barbara and Sybilla, in Leipzig. "It was a sort of gurgle, a *wrrau-wrrau-wrrau*—not like a whistle or a swish, but awful, like something very big cracking the air." It was her first experience with the dreaded phosphorus bombs.

No weapon in the Allied arsenal so terrified the civilian population. Christabel Bielenberg's most vivid memory of the Berlin raids was of "phosphorus bombs that burst and glowed green and emptied themselves down the walls and along the streets in flaming rivers of unquenchable flame, seeping down cellar stairs and sealing the exits to the air-raid shelters." In phosphorus attacks, great gusts of "air-raid wind" built to hurricane velocity as masses of cool air rushed to replace the superheated gases billowing upward. Trees were plucked from the ground and buses and streetcars were tossed about like toys in the resultant fire storms; people caught in them were swept into the heart of the conflagration and consumed.

Fear of phosphorus attack became almost an obsession after British and American bombers pounded the port city of Hamburg six times in nine days in late July and early August of 1943. Largely unopposed, the bombers went in first with high-explosive bombs that destroyed much of the city's water supply, then returned again and again to lay down incendiaries that showered the city with phosphorus pellets. In temperatures that reached 1,800° F., asphalt streets burst into flame and scorching winds swept over bomb shelters, incinerating those inside.

Some people got stuck in the melted asphalt and perished

for lack of oxygen. Others jumped into the Alster, the city's internal lake, to try to extinguish the smoldering phosphorus pellets embedded in their skin. But as soon as the victims emerged from the water the pellets began burning again, and many people died a lingering death as they alternated between burning alive and drowning. It was rumored that the Hamburg police had organized units of "hunting commandos" to find and shoot these unfortunates to put them out of their misery.

The nine-day toll was nearly 50,000 dead, 37,000 injured and almost half the city's buildings destroyed or damaged. Two thirds of Hamburg's 1.5 million inhabitants fled the battered city, spreading their tales of horror across the Reich. Irma Krueger, who lived in the town of Reinbek 11 miles away, recalled watching the endless column of dazed, soot-blackened refugees staggering down the main road. What struck her most was that they refused to stop, even when offered food and drink: "All they wanted to do was get away."

Weeks afterward, survivors were unable to describe the Hamburg raids without weeping hysterically. Throughout August, notices appeared in the provincial newspapers around Hamburg ordering policemen, railway workers, civil servants and party officials who had fled to return to their posts immediately. In his official report, the Hamburg Police Commissioner made no attempt at detachment. "No imagination," he wrote, "will ever be able to comprehend the scenes of terror."

The survivors of Hamburg began at once to rebuild, and within five months the city's production was back to 80 per cent of normal. Nevertheless, the devastating assault had frightened the Nazi leadership—"It put the fear of God into me," said Albert Speer—and it helped to change the party's

official response to the bombing campaign. Faced with the necessity of evacuating millions from endangered zones, party leaders stopped trying to conceal the raids from people in areas that had not yet been hit. There were no more claims that the Allies could not keep up the bombing; Göring and his staff talked less about the much-heavier blows the Luftwaffe supposedly was inflicting on the enemy. Even Goebbels had to concede that urban areas had become "a battlefront to a degree that the keenest foresight at the outset of the War could not have expected." But he insisted that the "air pirates" could not damage Germany's war potential, and the party quickly adopted this line in all its official pronouncements on the air offensive.

The mass evacuation of danger zones that began in the summer of 1943 unquestionably saved lives, but it created a new set of problems for both the government and the civilian population. Aside from the inhabitants of Hamburg and Berlin, most of the evacuees came from the hard-hit Rhineland cities and the Ruhr; they were sent to the farming districts of Bavaria, to Poland, the Baltic countries, eastern Germany and rural Austria, in particular the Alpine villages of the Tyrol.

At the outset, the government asked people in these so-called reception districts to take in evacuees voluntarily, but it quickly became apparent that this would not work. The Housing Commissioner of the Reich then authorized local authorities to appropriate space in houses and large apartments—with or without the owners' consent—and turn the space over to bombed-out persons. Inevitably, the order was resented. To the fiercely independent rural population, it seemed that the local Nazi functionaries—the "little Hitlers," as they were contemptuously called—were meddling in their private lives. On the evacuees' side, there was wide-

Like youngsters testing a new toy, Production Minister Albert Speer and two aides drive down a muddy slope on a hybrid tracked motorcycle developed in 1943. Speer subordinated Germany's consumer needs to the production of war matériel—in this case a vehicle to overcome "General Mud" on the Russian front.

spread suspicion that the evacuated wives and children of Nazi leaders were being given preferential billets.

Barely submerged social and regional prejudices and hatreds soon came to the surface. Berliners claimed that children evacuated from the smart West End of the city were favored over children from the working-class districts to the north. Bavarians recalled their old dislike of Prussians, and received them only with resentment and hostility. Residents of the rural Allgau asked why they had to take in refugees from the distant Ruhr instead of from Munich, where many of the villagers had relatives.

District administrators everywhere reported a basic mistrust between the people of town and country. Farmers complained that while they were toiling long hours in the fields without adequate help, the urban evacuees passed most of their time gossiping and complaining. In the farm communities, the common term for women evacuated from the Rhineland was "bomb wenches." The chief characteristic of these women, according to a report to the Appeals Court in Munich, was that "they indulge their laziness for months and, instead of working and helping the fatherland in its time of need, they turn the heads of farmers and flirt with them."

The evacuees, on the other hand, resented the fact that they were kept on strict rations while their hosts often had an abundance of food. One official report on the evacuation noted a common saying among evacuees that the farmers "eat like kings but live like pigs." Tension was further increased by rent-profiteering, which became commonplace in rural areas as wealthy evacuees tried to improve their quarters and local landlords took advantage of the situation. In the Tyrol, one room with a kitchen commanded as much as 600 marks a month—the equivalent of three months' wages for an average German industrial worker—along with a stipulated payment in tangible goods.

For Nazi officials at all levels, the evacuation was a constant source of worry. The secret service noted that Rhinelanders evacuated to the Tyrol were often influenced by the Catholic piety they encountered in the Alpine villages, leading them to question the party's official neopaganism and the correctness of its antireligious stand. At the same time, the party was concerned that evacuees in increasing numbers found the rural atmosphere so hostile that they were

fleeing back to the cities they had abandoned. The unauthorized drift became so serious that officials took to canceling the ration cards of people who returned, thereby precipitating riots at food offices.

A surprising number of city dwellers who went back to their homes did so because they missed the special camaraderie that developed among those under the bombs. "It was horrific, and I know it may sound foolish to say this," said Hilde Schott of Saarbrücken, "but people were never so friendly or so good again." Ursula von Kardorff wrote in her diary after fleeing to rural Bavaria that her "homesickness for Berlin, its fatalism, its generosity, its toughness, gets more and more acute." Whatever else the Allied bombing accomplished, it did not break civilian morale. Berliners were even able to joke about it, saying that the definition of cowardice was a Berliner who left for the front. "This disaster, which hits Nazis and anti-Nazis alike, is welding the people together," wrote Ursula von Kardorff, and many agreed. Barbara Knauth noted that the Leipzigers, who originally thought the camaraderie of Berliners, Hamburgers and Rhinelanders was affected, changed completely after they themselves had been bombed.

For a time, public sniping at the government subsided as the civilian population united in its hatred of the enemy. When Hitler declared before a largely female audience that he would retaliate a hundredfold against the British for every bomb dropped on the Reich, he was interrupted in midsentence by hysterical applause. But soon the regime's obvious inability to stop the raids led to even sharper criticism. Berliners took to saying "Now we can call him 'Meyer,'" an ironic reference to Göring's boast in 1939 that people could call him by the German-Jewish name "Meyer" if a bomb ever dropped on Berlin.

By the summer of 1943, the population had become so openly skeptical of official bulletins and predictions of all kinds that the OKW, the Armed Forces High Command, found it necessary to put up posters with the message, "For Everyone Knows the Truth is Brought/Only by the OKW Report." The public remained unconvinced. Despite Hitler's assurances in the spring that "I have taken all measures to assure victory in the coming months," few people believed the blandly optimistic bulletins on Rommel's deteriorating position in North Africa. Recalling an earlier boast by Hitler that no power on earth could dislodge the Germans from Stalingrad, people began talking about "Tunisgrad" long before the actual surrender of Axis forces in Tunisia in May. After the lightning Allied conquest of Sicily in July and August, there was open derision at an official communiqué that termed the Axis withdrawal a "defensive victory," even though the evacuation of German troops had indeed been carried out brilliantly.

The fall of Sicily followed close on the collapse of the Fascist dictatorship in Italy and the ouster of Mussolini, events that badly shook both the Nazi leadership and German public opinion. Then in early September the Allies breached Hitler's allegedly impregnable Fortress Europe with landings in southern Italy. A month later, Hitler issued an order of the day to his armies in the East commanding them to maintain a defensive line along the Dnieper River. Party newspapers were hardly on the street with the boast that "the general offensive of the enemy has been stopped" before Soviet troops crossed the Dnieper in several places.

As one piece of bad news followed another, Nazi propaganda began claiming that a defensive war was a sign that Germany was strong enough to be able to wait while the enemy made costly mistakes. Even retreat was explained as being part of a grand plan to lure the Red Army to its doom. The newspaper *Das Schwarze Korps* insisted that in accordance with the "strategy of wide spaces," no position was held "an hour longer than necessary from an exclusively military point of view. Our military command can nicely separate questions of prestige and strategy."

But privately the party leadership admitted an increasing inability to convince the public. Instead of accepting official explanations, said one internal report, people were now reading between the lines and trying to ascertain the truth from nuances of language. It became widely known, for example, that a flattering citation of a unit at the front generally meant that the unit had been destroyed; friends called Ursula von Kardorff to commiserate after her brother's division in the East was lauded in an Army communiqué. People now expressed a grudging admiration for Churchill as a man who "told his nation the truth." The general distrust of official propaganda was summed up in a popular joke: A man attending services at Cologne Cathedral meets a friend who is carrying a radio. "Why the radio?" he asks. "Because," says his friend, "it has told too many lies and needs to go to confession."

As 1943 gave way to 1944, the Allies extended the range of their bombing to cities in the south of Germany such as Munich and Nuremberg, which hitherto had remained virtually untouched. In the Württemberg-Baden region alone, more than 40,000 lives were lost and 130,000 houses and apartments were destroyed. "I shall never forget, even if I live to be 100, how the Royal Air Force turned our beloved Nuremberg into ash and rubble," recalled Fritz Weidmann, a schoolboy at the time. Others would have liked to forget but could not. A Munich policeman was haunted for years by the memory of digging out 14 adults who had tried until their air gave out to claw their way free: "When we found them, their faces distorted by terror, all of them had their fingers worn down to the very bone!"

With virtually the entire country suffering from the bombing, remarkably frank personal testimonies began to appear in the press. In February of 1944 an anonymous fire fighter described in a party newspaper how he felt after a raid: "We are empty of emotion. Our heads ring and our legs are like rubber. Food is brought up. In silence we swallow the bread and sausage. It tastes of burning. Someone comes up and reports that five of our comrades are dead. We listen without comment." The fireman found a phone and called home to learn if his house was still standing and his wife still alive: "I dial our number with my heart beating furiously. I wait for my wife's voice. Nothing! In silence I return to my group. We clamber on the back of a truck and fall asleep immediately."

Such apathy afflicted many of the survivors. Relief workers arriving in the devastated cities from the outside were struck by the sight of people sitting motionless among the ruins of their homes or wandering like sleepwalkers through the streets clutching some household belonging, a lampshade or a flower vase. They were given soup, clothing and footwear by the mobile relief columns that toured the Reich constantly, manned by Army personnel, and by Red Cross workers and members of the National Socialist Women's Organization. Tents were provided for emergency housing until something else became available.

Once the initial shock wore off, the streets of the bombed cities became so thronged with scurrying people that Sybilla Knauth in Leipzig was reminded of "an ant heap that has been stirred up with a stick." Everywhere, she recalled, "people walked and walked, carrying things out, carrying things back in, carting off rubbish." And there was a peculiar smell that hung over the ruins, Hildegarde Neff remembered—"the smell of burning and the sweet, fatty smell of the buried, not yet dug out."

Some people never got used to the horrors; others came to accept them with a kind of numbness that surprised even themselves.

A woman in Mainz crawled out of her cellar after a raid to look for food and saw rescue workers "laying out the pathetic, twisted bodies of several children." She was overcome by the sight, and by the thought that "they had never really had any life; all their years on earth there had been shortage and war." At that, "all hunger fled," and she turned and went back to her cellar.

Ursula von Kardorff, on the other hand, became "so used to the presence of death" that when she went to a dinner party in Berlin after a raid, she realized only while eating that two doors away the tappings of people suffocating under the rubble of the Hotel Bristol could still be faintly heard. What appalled her afterward, she noted in her diary, was that "we went on eating and drinking and making polite conversation" as if the horror did not exist.

Many cities were now just shells, with people living like cave dwellers among the ruins. By the beginning of 1944, Germany lacked an estimated 11 million dwellings. People recalled that when Robert Ley assumed responsibility for civilian housing he had promised airy, sunny homes for all Germans. Survivors of the terror raids joked bitterly, "Well, now we have all the sun and air we need."

Looking over the devastation of Hamburg, a Frau Wolff-Monckeberg felt that "I must talk about this, the fifth winter of the War." In a letter that she never mailed, she described the "heaps of rubble wherever one looks, hollow ruins of houses, empty windows, lonely chimney stacks, charred remnants of furniture, high up on a bit of a wall a bathtub, a forlorn bedframe, a radiator or even a picture clinging precariously to the bombed-out shell of what was once someone's home." Mountains of garbage were accumulating in the streets: "Then the wind takes it all and scatters it over the wet roads, leaving a stale, foul stench." She wondered sadly if this could really be "our super modern and clean Hamburg."

In the absence of able-bodied men, the youth of Germany now came to the aid of the shattered cities. They served as messengers, telephone operators, hospital orderlies, rescue diggers, fire fighters and ultimately as antiaircraft gunners. Some 700,000 teenagers of the Hitler Youth were enlisted in civil defense. When the 16-year-old boys disappeared into the infantry, their positions in the antiaircraft batteries were filled by teenagers recruited from the League of German Girls.

Young people of both sexes exhibited a courage—and sometimes a fanaticism—that impressed even party leaders. One teen-age girl rushed from a basement into the flaming streets of Darmstadt and asked a man with a swastika arm band to lend her his gas mask so she could dig out people overcome by smoke. When the man refused either to give her his mask or to go into the cellars himself, she tore the swastika from his arm, enraged that "someone who wore this badge could be such a coward." Braving the flames without a mask, she and a 14-year-old boy began bringing people out of the ruins and ferrying them to the hospital on the handlebars of a bicycle. The girl later explained her matter-of-fact heroism by saying she belonged to the generation that "had learned early not to ask questions but to get on with the job."

During the early months of 1944, Allied fighter planes —Spitfires, Lightnings, Thunderbolts and Mustangs—were equipped with auxiliary fuel tanks that enabled them to accompany the heavy bombers on strikes deep into Germany. A new kind of air war began as the fighters and fighter-bombers—"the low-fliers," the Germans called them— came winging in at treetop level, cannon and machine guns blazing, to add to the terror of the heavy bombers.

A prime target of the low-fliers was local trains. In the rural Eifel area south of Bonn, little distinction was made between military trains and civilian trains loaded with students and with farmers returning from market. Civilian casualties rose, and so did outrage at this kind of warfare, which somehow seemed more personal because the pilot and the people he was strafing could see each other. Goebbels took advantage of the public's anger by publishing two articles in the party press in the spring of 1944 demanding that downed strafers be killed like mad dogs. Although Goebbels received many letters of support, the public ignored his advice. Except for an isolated incident in which farmers near the village of Spicheren in the Eifel beat a bomber pilot to death, Germany's rural population treated captured fliers remarkably well.

A secret-service report in the spring of 1944 noted that female farm workers were refusing to go into the fields for fear they would be attacked by low-flying aircraft. The mood in the rural areas following such attacks was said to be much like that in the cities: The people were interested only in survival. Almost no one believed that the bombing offensive could be stopped or that anything short of a miracle could save Germany.

In fact, something close to a miracle had begun to occur late in 1943, when Albert Speer assumed control of industrial production. By radically curtailing the consumer industry, allocating labor and raw materials more shrewdly, and

dispersing factories to rural areas to remove them from air attack, Speer managed, amazingly, to increase German war production even while German cities were being bombed around the clock. After tripling the output of single-engined fighter planes, he confidently told Hitler in 1944 that the nation's stock of war goods was sufficient to last another year.

But the public was little interested in production figures. Increasingly, Nazi propaganda hinted that a miracle weapon was being produced that would change the course of the War. Hitler himself boasted that "technical and systematic preconditions are being created" that would enable him to retaliate against England "with other and more effective means." Desperate for reassurance of any kind, people both believed in the possibility of a wonder weapon and scoffed at it. There were wild rumors of an aircraft so fast it had to fire backward so as not to run into its own missiles, and of gigantic compressed-air pumps that could scatter a division like chaff. On the other hand, Berliners joked that the British were dropping hay on the city for the jackasses who still believed in a new weapon of revenge.

When Germany's V-1 buzz bombs began hitting London on the 13th of June, 1944, followed shortly by the more sophisticated V-2 rockets, many people believed the wonder weapons had arrived. The news even dispelled some of the anxieties Germans were feeling about the D-Day landings in Normandy, which had taken place just a week earlier. "We were almost crazy with joy," recalled party worker Fritz Muehlebach. "There was panic in London, the town was in flames, and we saw again how the Führer had kept his word." But Muehlebach's joy was short-lived. Soon the Allied armies were fanning out from the Normandy beachhead, progressively depriving the Wehrmacht of the V-1 and V-2 launching sites it needed to sustain the bombardment of England.

After D-Day, German civilians enjoyed a brief respite from the air offensive as bombers were diverted to the Normandy front. When the bombers came back late in the summer, it was in heavier force than ever. With the German transport system now under general attack, rail travel became all but impossible. Christabel Bielenberg recalled a journey from the Black Forest to Berlin that should have taken several hours but instead took four days, during which the train was attacked by dive bombers and sat for long peri-

Newly decorated flak helpers, wounded while defending Munich against an Allied air raid in 1943, attend a funeral for comrades who died in the attack. The older boys in Hitler Youth antiaircraft units operated the guns while the younger ones—some were only 11 or 12 years old— manned searchlights or served as messengers.

ods in tunnels, waiting for enemy planes to pass. The last lap of the journey had to be made on foot because all traffic into Berlin had been cut off.

Merely getting on a train was nightmarishly difficult. Civilians queued up for hours to obtain the few tickets that had not been reserved for soldiers or for officials traveling on war business. To be on hand when the erratic trains arrived, travelers spent days and nights camping in the stations. Cars were so overcrowded that some people got aboard by clambering through windows. One passenger who fought her way onto the Munich-Berlin express encountered a scene of "indescribable confusion: I had my dress half torn off me, my shoes spoiled. I was kissed by the soldier nearest to me and could not resist because I had my arms pinned to my sides."

When a freight train stopped because of an air-raid alert, looters immediately swarmed over it. One of Ilse McKee's bitterest memories was of wrestling a bag of potatoes from a crowd of fellow looters on a stalled train outside Leipzig, only to have it stolen when she took shelter from a strafing attack. "I sat down on the pavement and cried," she re-

called. Young Irma Krueger found herself in the contrary situation after pedaling to a damaged food depot some 15 miles from her home and discovering it was "swarming with adults, fighting for bags of sugar." She was about to give up when RAF fighters appeared and swept the area with machine-gun fire. As the crowd scattered, she hoisted a 100-pound bag of sugar onto the handlebars of her bicycle and made off "with bullets whizzing about everywhere." She arrived home with her tires ruined but the sugar intact; bartered on the black market for food, the sugar kept her family going for weeks.

With food trains arriving sporadically if at all, people took to foraging for anything they could find to eat. Often they took hair-raising chances. Klaus Ritter, who lived in the border region of the Eifel, remembered going out with friends under a protective cover of fog to see if they could find a grazing cow to slaughter. They quickly discovered that the meadows were littered with the carcasses of cows that had been blown up by land mines buried as part of the German defenses. Deciding their hunger was more urgent than the danger of stepping on a mine, they went on gingerly search-

ing until they came upon a grazing cow. Ritter reported that it made a "juicy roast."

In the midst of their struggle for survival, many Germans began asking who or what was responsible for the horrors around them. The question became so insistent that the head of the propaganda office in Berlin wrote to a colleague about it on June 2, 1944: "One learns in talks with the public and from conversations in air-raid shelters that the belief frequently exists that Germany carries a certain measure of responsibility for the outbreak of war in 1939, and the burdens and worries of this war were therefore to a considerable extent the fault of the Reich."

Goebbels was so alarmed by this attitude that he wrote an article for *Das Reich* titled "Was This War Avoidable?" His argument was that Germany's enemies had been preparing for war for years, and that if the Wehrmacht had not struck when it did, sooner or later Germany would have been the victim of a surprise attack. The enemy's aim was not to bring down the party, wrote Goebbels, but to "exterminate us as a people."

This identification of the people with the party became a staple of Nazi propaganda once it became apparent that the Allies were winning the War. In speeches and in articles, officials of the party insisted that the enemy would hold every German responsible for the rigors of the Occupation and the devastation that had occurred in Italy and in the East. Posters proclaimed "Victory or ruin" and "Victory or Bolshevist chaos."

At the same time, penalties for defeatism were made more severe, and much public emphasis was put on the extermination of "enemies of the people." In one case that attracted wide attention, 17 postal employees in Vienna were publicly executed for stealing chocolates from gift packages intended for soldiers at the front.

By 1944, death sentences were being imposed on youngsters 14 to 16 years old. Goebbels warned that "whoever infringes on Germany's security is a dead man." A Berlin pastor was executed for telling an anti-Nazi joke, a married couple for counseling their son to cultivate a bladder in-

fection in order to escape military service, a manufacturer for "defeatist utterances to business acquaintances," a pensioner for taking a pair of trousers he found lying beside a bombed-out house, a tradesman for "unusually subversive utterances at an inn."

When the Nazi leadership launched a third, desperate Total Mobilization in July of 1944, somehow scraping up an additional 630,000 workers for the armaments industry, the one obvious source of manpower on the home front that was not tapped was the Nazi terror apparatus. In fact, the party let it be known that the terror machine would be enlarged. A dreaded People's Court under the notorious Judge Roland Freisler now convened in almost continuous session, with condemnations to death virtually assured before the trials began.

Yet the Nazis were powerless to halt the erosion of will and morale that the leaders saw with alarm on every side. The public prosecutor of Bamberg noted that more people were listening to enemy radio broadcasts and that fewer regarded it as a punishable offense—even though it constituted "moral self-mutilation" and automatically placed them in the category of "enemies of the people." A newspaper in northern Germany estimated that millions of Germans listened to the enemy every night, despite heavy Gestapo pressure to prevent it.

Even more disturbing was the disappearance of Nazi Party badges from lapels, and the replacement of the words *"Heil Hitler!"* by more traditional German greetings. Eventually, SS Chief Heinrich Himmler issued an order requiring party members to wear their badges and uniforms at all times. And a party newspaper scolded its readers: "Years ago you could not shout *'Heil Hitler!'* loudly enough; today your greeting is just an indistinct mumble. Years ago you could not stretch your arms up high enough; today you make just a vague gesture." Gauleiter Paul Wegener of Bremen admonished in a similar vein: "Now that Hitler's ship has run into stormy weather, many turn green and blue with seasickness and would like to disembark." But it was too late to avoid the storm.

In a dogged pretense of normality, Christmas decorations and a sign heralding a holiday sale festoon a bomb-damaged Cologne street in December of 1944. By that time, most household commodities were reserved for sale to victims of air raids.

LIFE UNDER THE BOMBS

ENDURING AN ENDLESS RAIN OF MISERY

For three years, beginning in 1942, the cities of Germany endured a campaign of strategic bombing unprecedented in human history. By night, British bombers flew so-called saturation raids that were as unselectively ruinous as the name suggests. By day, waves of American planes sought to pinpoint important military and industrial targets, but their bombs sometimes struck homes or office buildings instead. As many as 1,600 bombers roared over a city in a single raid; often they returned a day later—and again and again until it seemed to beleaguered Germans that the bombing never stopped. Official estimates of the bomb tonnage that fell on Germany begin at one million tons. The bombs wiped out more than 11 million dwellings and an estimated half million civilian lives.

The average air-raid shelter—a cellar in a house or business establishment—provided uncertain protection. A direct hit on the structure above might cave in the shelter and crush everyone within it. Or the refugees might survive the bombs and the wreckage above, only to be trapped below-ground and die of asphyxiation. For those who remained aboveground during a raid to muster what defenses they could against the relentless pummeling, the terrors were manifold. Among the worst were incendiary bombs, which ignited on impact and spread fire everywhere. "I saw people tearing off their clothes as they caught fire," a survivor recalled. When the Allied bombers dropped incendiaries in quantity—and in a typical raid, a half million were dropped—they generated fire storms. These moving towers of flame reached a mind-boggling 1,800° F., and tore through the streets with a shrill howl that one German remembered as "terrible music."

By the end of 1944, Berlin alone had experienced 24 major raids, and Germans everywhere felt their cities had been bombed into a new Stone Age. "There was no water, no light, no fire," one survivor recalled. Thousands of city dwellers fled, but most stayed where they were, clinging stubbornly to what was left of their homes, and doggedly getting on with life in the midst of destruction.

Photographed from above, a British Lancaster bomber is silhouetted in the sky over Hamburg amid patterns of tracer bullets, flak and ground fires.

Interrupted by air-raid sirens during an afternoon stroll, citizens of Berlin evacuate a city park. When a raid caught them away from home and their designated neighborhood shelters, civilians crowded into public bunkers and subway stations.

Carrying blankets for warmth and a radio to keep her informed, a German woman and her children clamber down the steps of a cellar tunnel as two men follow behind

Hesitantly smiling, women and children while away the night in an air-raid shelter. Women with small children to round up found the sudden alerts particularly distressing to be on the safe side they began gathering at the shelters at 6 o'clock in the evening

By the light of a kerosene lamp, a woman mends as her companion reads a book during long hours in a shelter. Many cities called alerts as soon as Allied planes were reported crossing the English Channel. In Cologne there were nine alerts for every actual raid.

earchlights and showers of antiaircraft tracer fire make an eerie
ackdrop for the twin spires of Cologne Cathedral during a raid. Though
it repeatedly by incendiary and high-explosive bombs, the cathedral
—parts of which were 600 years old—miraculously survived the War.

As a Munich couple run for shelter with a few belongings in their arms, firemen fight the blaze raging behind them. Approximately 150,000 persons were employed full time in fire fighting throughout Germany.

Shouldering shovels, men of the National Labor Service march between a burning building and some jettisoned household effects to begin the work of cleaning up. The piles of rubble sometimes reached as high as the second story of surviving buildings.

Distressed civilians pause in a bombed-out street in Berlin. One German remembered that people "staggered like sleepwalkers" after a raid.

Hitler Youths hose down a smoldering city building. Boys as young as 10 were enlisted in the work of cleaning up following a raid.

Walking through the city after an air raid, one Berliner wears a helmet as protection against falling ash while another holds a handkerchief in his mouth. Often the ash and smoke were so dense that, as one woman lamented, "the air just didn't come."

In a Hamburg bomb shelter, Germans lie dead from carbon monoxide poisoning. The gas, which resulted from incomplete combustion, accounted for up to 80 per cent of incendiary-bomb casualties.

Using a makeshift device of rope and planks, rescue workers remove the crushed body of a Duisburg resident from a collapsed ruin.

The charred remains of an air-raid sentry and his bicycle lie on a Hamburg street, where a fire storm incinerated them. Fire storms could travel with the speed of wind and follow a course as erratic as that of a tornado.

Incongruously decked with Christmas trees, a Berlin gym serves as a temporary morgue in December 1944. In the last year and a half of the War, 77,750 civilians reported missing throughout Germany were never found.

medical equipment. Every hospital was identified by a large red cross on its roof. But according to an official Allied survey, the cross became ''no longer a shield of safety but a pinpoint for pilots over a city.''

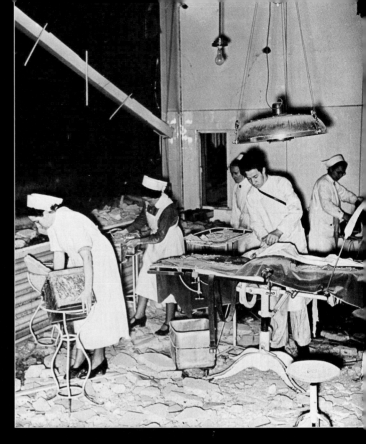

Berliners shovel industriously to clear the streets after a 1944 air raid. In spite of their efforts, the mounds of debris grew in number and size, prompting many Germans to joke grimly that ''Berlin will be in the Alps.''

Residents of Cologne scavenge for preserved fruit.   At a makeshift kitchen of coal-burning stoves, homeless Berliners cook a meal in the street.

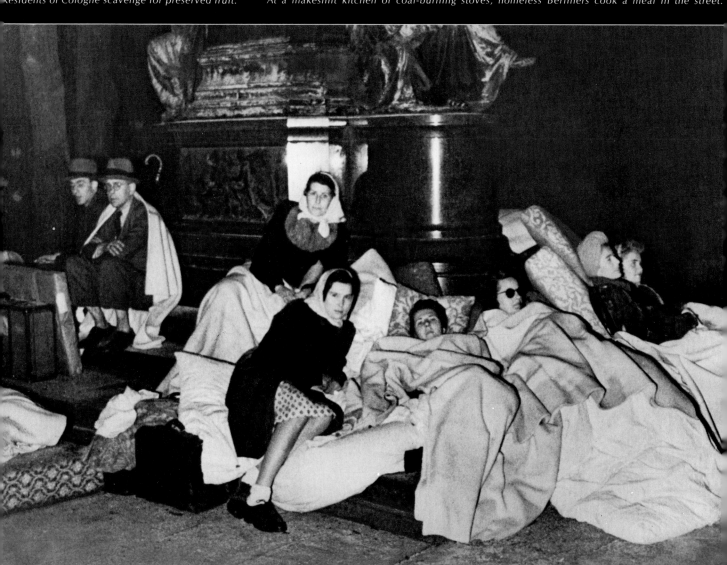

At the base of a city monument, Düsseldorfers bed down for a night. "We have nothing to worry about now," one said bitterly. "We have nothing left at all."

On Hamburg's Marienstrasse, clogged with fire hoses, members of the National Labor Service help residents salvage furniture from buildings made uninhabitable by smoke and water damage. Almost one million Hamburgers were left homeless by the air raids.

Under a sign saying "Sieg"—"victory"—refugees line up in a Hamburg railway station. "We went like gypsies out of our dear burning town," one woman recalled. The exodus was so massive that Hamburg was temporarily left short of police and civil servants to run the city.

At a municipal office in Berlin, bombed-out citizens wait for passes to leave the city in late 1944.

urrounded by debris and bathed in sunlight from an open roof, citizens of Cologne worship in a bombed church.

transportation — and overlooking class distinctions — officers, businessmen and laborers in Berlin head for their day's work, riding aboard motor-drawn trail

In a poignant gesture to tradition, a man places a wreath on a Cologne rubble heap at Christmas time, 1944. His family lay dead and buried under the wreckage.

Viewed from the bell tower of St. Nicholas Church, the medieval quarter of Hamburg presents a bleak spectacle. Among the casualties of Allied bombing in this city alone were 17 historic churches, six theaters and many people—40,000 in one terrible week.

5

"Turn on the wireless, turn on the wireless; they've thrown a bomb at Hitler!" Christabel Bielenberg was returning from a walk through the Black Forest village of Rohrbach when a neighbor greeted her with the shocking news. The English-born Frau Bielenberg, married to a German, had moved to Rohrbach from Berlin with her three children in 1943 to avoid the air raids and chronic food shortages that beset the capital. "Yes, yes, go on," she responded to the neighbor, trying her best not to shout. "What happened, have they succeeded?" "I don't know," replied the neighbor, "but it's all being said on the wireless."

"I ran through the kitchen to the parlor with my heart thumping," recalled Frau Bielenberg, "and waited for the elderly contraption to warm up. Goebbels was speaking—not Goebbels, it did not matter, the same suave voice. The wireless said that a coup attempt had been made on the life of the Leader, by some generals whose names I had heard but did not know."

Thus did Christabel Bielenberg learn on July 20, 1944, of the plot by a group of Army officers and several civilians to assassinate Hitler. The plotters had placed a bomb in Hitler's headquarters in East Prussia. When the bomb exploded, it killed Hitler's official stenographer and wounded nearly a score of others, three of whom later died. But Hitler himself suffered only minor injuries. That night a triumphant Führer addressed the nation by radio, gloating that his escape was "a confirmation of my assignment from Providence to continue my life's goal." He then unleashed a savage campaign of retribution in which nearly 5,000 people eventually were executed.

In the wake of the assassination attempt, agents of the SD were sent out to gauge the mood of the people. The agents were instructed to be candid in their reports, which were to be read only by the nation's leaders. They frankly expected to find many Germans—worn down by five years of war and increasing privations—reacting to the assassination attempt much as did non-German Christabel Bielenberg, who asked in dismay: "How did it fail; why did it fail?" But so strong was the Führer's hold on his *Volk*, reported the SD agents, that "even elements of the population who are not out-and-out supporters of National Socialism detest the attempted assassination; we found a large number of such reactions from northern districts of Berlin that had stood in

TWILIGHT OF THE REICH

clear opposition before. They exclaimed that it was a foul act to stab Hitler in the back that way.''

Among those who had always supported Hitler, noted an official who compiled the SD reports, the reaction was one of ''sudden dismay, emotional shock and anger.'' From several cities, he wrote, ''there are reports of women bursting into tears in stores and on the streets, some completely out of control. Heaving a sigh of relief, the public responded, 'Thank God the Führer is alive.' ''

Hitler was buoyed by the SD reports. He confided to Albert Speer, his personal architect and Minister for Armaments and War Production, that the plotters' misdeed signaled a turning point in German history, one that would yet lead to a German triumph. Very soon, however, it became apparent that the Wehrmacht could stop neither the massive Anglo-American force that had landed in France on June 6 nor the Red Army that was now surging through Poland at an alarming speed. Hitler retreated to a more cynical view of the situation. ''If the German nation is defeated in this struggle,'' he told a meeting of gauleiters, ''it has been too weak. This will mean it has not withstood the test of history and was destined for nothing but doom.''

With that gloomy pronouncement—one that he would sound over and over in the waning days of the War—Hitler disappeared into his bunker in Berlin, as if its concrete roof, 16 feet thick, could shield him from the increasingly gloomy news: the Allies' liberation of Paris in late August and the Red Army's entrance into Bucharest at about the same time. In the bunker, which reminded Speer of an ancient Egyptian tomb, Hitler could dream of a miracle victory while ''locked up inside his delusions.'' There was no such escape from reality for the German people, however. As the Allies advanced on two fronts, SD agents reported ''a new low in morale,'' concluding that ''the assessment of our position has caused dejection and widespread hopelessness as never before in five years of war.''

Home-front morale suffered another blow in late October when American troops captured and occupied Aachen, near the western border. It was the first sizable German city to fall—and a portent of things to come. By the first month of the new year, millions of Germans would be living under Anglo-American occupation in western Germany. At the same time in eastern Germany, the Red Army would estab-lish bridgeheads across the Oder River—positioning itself less than 40 miles from Berlin.

If further proof was needed that the Third Reich was in its death throes, British and American bombers supplied it in February of 1945 by unleashing a fire storm in the city of Dresden that burned for seven days. Symbolically Dresden, renowned for the gilded splendor of its baroque architecture, was the funeral pyre for Adolf Hitler's empire. The conflagration—followed by Hitler's order to his armies to scorch German earth as they retreated—set the stage for an ending reminiscent of one of the Führer's favorite Wagnerian operas: After 12 years of Nazi rule, *Götterdämmerung*—the Twilight of the Gods—was at hand.

On September 11, 1944, an American patrol crossed from Luxembourg into Germany near the village of Stolzembourg. By the following morning the American First Army of General Courtney Hodges, half a million strong, was advancing inside the Reich along a 60-mile front. Directly in the line of the American advance stood the city of Aachen, known to the French as Aix-la-Chapelle and to the Dutch as Aken. The Germans had long revered Aachen as the burial site of Charlemagne, mightiest of the early Germanic kings.

In modern times, the city of 160,000 was noted for its mineral waters and hot sulfur baths. On the outskirts of Aachen were factories that produced pins and needles, glass, tires and textiles. These factories already had come under severe attack by the Allies, as had Aachen itself. By late 1944, seventy-five large-scale air raids had destroyed almost half of the city's buildings and badly damaged most of the rest; three quarters of the population had fled the city in search of safer ground. For all that, shattered Aachen still had to be defended. Psychologically, the loss of a shrine-city that played a significant role in National Socialist mythology would be devastating. Militarily, the city was an important link in the string of fortifications known as the West Wall that ran from Holland to Switzerland.

When news of the American advance reached Aachen, panic set in among the 40,000 civilians still living there. All over the city, people gathered whatever creature comforts they could carry and took shelter in bunkers and basements. Local party leaders—derisively known as ''Golden Pheasants'' because of their fondness for gold braid—fled to the town of Jülich, 20 miles away, leaving Aachen's inhabitants to fend for themselves. At the same time, hundreds of Wehrmacht troops broke into the vast cellars of the city's foremost wine dealer and appropriated the stock, setting off a drunken orgy of looting and vandalism.

It appeared that Aachen would be taken almost without a fight. But Hitler had other ideas; he ordered the evacuation of the city's remaining civilians, and he sent one of his best commanders—Major General Gerhard Graf von Schwerin—to lead its defense.

Schwerin arrived in the city from France on September 12, along with the remains of his division, the 116th Panzer, which had been mauled in the course of the Allied invasion. Schwerin was given additional men to defend Aachen, but they were a decidedly motley lot. Among them were several "stomach" and "ear-and-throat" battalions—sickly soldiers grouped together by ailment so they could be treated more handily—and members of the *Volkssturm*, teen-age striplings and old men with little military training.

In the chaos of the moment, Schwerin was probably uncertain how many troops he actually had under his command. But as he drove through Aachen past columns of fleeing civilians, Schwerin—whom Hitler thought of as "a splendid battlefield commander who unfortunately is not a National Socialist"—had few illusions that he could stop the Americans. At best he might be able to slow them north of Aachen, a move he knew would leave the southern approaches undefended and allow the Americans to take the city proper without further destruction or bloodshed.

"How many civilians are there?" he asked an aide at his headquarters in the once elegant Hotel Quellenhof. "It is hard to say, sir," he was told. "Perhaps 40,000." Schwerin nodded. "Make an announcement that I, as battle commander of Aachen, order that there be no further attempt to evacuate the city."

The following day, as the sound of enemy artillery grew louder, Schwerin wrote a note, in English, to the as-yet-unidentified enemy commander. "I stopped the absurd evacuation of this town," he wrote; "therefore I am responsible for the fate of its inhabitants, and I ask you to take care of the unfortunate population in a humane way." Schwerin handed the note to a postal official—one of the few bureaucrats who had not fled—and told the man to hand the note to the first American officer he encountered.

Schwerin then took up new headquarters in a farmhouse outside Aachen, where he spent a restless night waiting for word that the Americans had occupied the city. Instead, he learned that the enemy's tanks had been slowed by the great forests and tank traps south of Aachen. To add to Schwerin's problems, his commanding officer, General Friedrich Au-

gust Schack, had ordered him to speed up the civilian evacuation that—unbeknownst to his superiors—he had halted.

The next day, a unit of Storm Troopers arrived and began herding the remaining civilians into columns heading east. "Only those people may remain in Aachen who have a place in the coming battle," proclaimed the Storm Trooper commander, a Major Zimmermann. "All others will be moved—without mercy." Schwerin knew that his plan to save what was left of Aachen had failed. Furthermore, someone had discovered his letter to the Americans.

"It can only be a matter of hours before you are relieved of command," General Schack told Schwerin in a curt telephone conversation. "Please place yourself at my disposal." Instead, Schwerin went into hiding for six days, protected by a motorcycle detachment of loyal troops who had sworn to fight rather than allow the arrest of their general.

General von Schwerin—who eventually did surrender and was let off with a reprimand for his disobedience instead of the death sentence he had expected—was not the only one to go into hiding. All over the ruined city, thousands of Aacheners had decided to do the same: People burned their Nazi Party uniforms and badges, gave the Storm Troopers hunting them the slip, and hid in cellars and bombed-out buildings. On the outskirts of Aachen, several farmers refused to be forced from their homes; a few barricaded themselves inside their houses and fired on the German troops trying to evict them. Similar scenes were repeated all along the path of the American advance. In the village of Saarlautern, 100 miles south of Aachen, 1,700 people hid in a nearby mine rather than be evacuated. And in Würselen, five miles northeast of Aachen, 4,000 townspeople managed to hide from the evacuation troops, who were under orders to shoot any stragglers.

To all those who hid in and around Aachen, the end of the War seemed near. To be transported deeper into the Reich—where many more months of bombing and privation were likely—seemed a poor alternative to surrender. So, for the next six weeks thousands of Aacheners cowered underground as two armies fought for their shattered city.

Wilhelm Savelsberg, a 53-year-old streetcar motorman, was typical of those who chose to wait out the battle for Aachen rather than flee. With his wife, their daughter-in-law and an infant, he hid in the cellar of a ruined building. Savelsberg lived by his wits; he managed to round up a small menagerie of abandoned animals that he used to feed his family, including a cow that he kept in a nearby shed and milked at night. During the day, the Savelsbergs tried to stay out of sight. But they could not hide all the time; for one thing, the baby's diapers needed laundering, something that could not be done in the cellar. Thus they had to venture outside, risking fire from Germans and Americans alike.

The besieged family tried to solve that problem by hanging a white flag in the ruined upper story of their building every time they hung out their wash, hoping that the combatants would respect it and hold their fire. One morning two German soldiers spotted the flag and angrily ordered the Savelsberg women to take it down.

"We have to protect ourselves," the women responded.

"Have it your own way!" one of the soldiers shouted back. "But tomorrow I'll see to it that the police collect you two whores!"

As the soldiers walked away, American artillery opened up, blasting the spot where they had been standing. A short time later, Wilhelm Savelsberg crept into the street to make sure the two had been killed. If they had survived and reported the women, the family would have to flee or face the consequences—prison or a firing squad. As he inched his way down the ruined street, American artillery started up once more, and Savelsberg scurried for shelter. When the shelling ceased Savelsberg could find no trace of the two soldiers, but he concluded that if the first salvo had not killed them, the ensuing ones surely had. His family was not reported; they survived the remaining weeks of the battle by foraging for food in abandoned houses.

A family named Baurmann lived an even more harrowing existence than the Savelsbergs, holed up in a farmhouse only 200 yards from the stalled American lines. There, in the cellar of what became known as "the last house in Aachen," Frau Doris Baurmann, her six children, her young aunt and Maria Kalff, her mother-in-law, lived through the thick of the fighting. Grandmother Kalff, a stern, white-haired woman whose family called her "the High Command" behind her back, kept the family going—organizing scavenging expeditions for food and water and shooing off any German soldiers who came near.

Carrying what they can—including a white flag asking for safe passage—German women, children and an old man hurry from desolated Aachen after its fall to the U.S. First Army on the 21st of October, 1944. The Americans set up camps outside Aachen to feed and shelter the thousands left homeless by the 39-day battle to capture the border city.

Once, when a Wehrmacht lieutenant tried to set up his command post in her home, she told him that things were too dangerous in the area, that the air contained "too much metal." Almost as if on cue, enemy machine guns opened fire, and the officer retreated. Eventually some friendly German soldiers took the Baurmann family under their wing, discouraging patrols that were searching the dying city for civilians. "Who would want to live within 200 yards of the American lines?" they would ask the searchers innocently.

At nearby Würselen, many of the townspeople escaped detection by organizing a lookout system. A guard who spotted someone in uniform would whistle, and his fellow civilians would hurry off to another subterranean hideout—where they lived, as one villager noted, "together with and in the company of mice."

By the afternoon of October 16, American troops had surrounded Aachen. Still, the city was far from subdued. Its defenders turned every street into a battleground, forcing the Americans to take the place one block at a time. A correspondent for Czech émigré newspapers in London was with the Americans as they fought for Aachen. In the wake of their advance, he reported, the civilians who had refused to be evacuated began to emerge from their shelters. They were, he said, "the drabbest, filthiest inhabitants of the underworld I have ever seen. People came stumbling out into the light, dazed, then catching a breath of fresh air and finally starting to jabber, push, scream and curse."

The correspondent went on: "It was a stunning sight. These were the people of the first German town occupied by the Allies. And they were weeping with hysterical joy among the smoldering ruins of their homes. 'We have been praying for you to come,' said a woman with a pale, thin face. 'You can't imagine what we have had to suffer.' "

A short time later, a squad of GIs came upon a plump, grimy man in the streets. Summoning all his dignity, the man—who looked remarkably like an unkempt Winston Churchill—stared his captors in the eye and announced, "I am Johannes van der Velden, the Bishop of Aachen." The startled Americans radioed their headquarters for advice on what to do with a captured bishop. "Treat him like a general," they were told.

That was better treatment than civilians in German-held parts of the city were receiving from their own soldiers as the fight for Aachen raged on. "The officers stopped us from talking to the civilians," recalled one German soldier, "and orders were given to fire on any civilian trying to leave the city." An Aachener who managed to evade Wehrmacht bullets remembered the soldiers yelling at him, "If we have to die, you can die, too." The result, according to one observer, was "a hatred that you find only in civil wars."

Early on October 21, Colonel Gerhard Wilck—who had replaced General von Schwerin as the commander of Aachen—decided to surrender, despite his fear that his wife and children might be executed if he did. "It was," he recalled, "the most difficult decision of my life." The act of surrender itself was far from simple; in the fighting near

Hiding from both American artillery and Nazi Storm Troopers, civilians gather for a meal (left) in an abandoned mine near Saarlautern. At top, some of the mine's 1,700 inhabitants venture out of the entrance after American troops had driven off the Storm Troopers, who were threatening to entomb the refugees for their refusal to evacuate to the east.

Wilck's command bunker, two German officers carrying a white flag were shot. Thirty captured Americans were being held inside the bunker. Wilck asked for volunteers to accompany an English-speaking German officer under a flag of truce. It was a smart move. When the American troops saw two GIs leading a German officer, they held their fire.

Within minutes the officer was behind American lines relaying Wilck's desire to capitulate. At noon that day, Wilck surrendered; the long battle was over. The Reich had lost an important city and had suffered a grave psychological blow, for Hitler had vowed that Aachen would never be taken. Its fall was a signal that Germany, which had ruled so much of Europe, was about to feel the heel of the conqueror.

As American forces took over Aachen, reported a correspondent traveling with them, "German civilians are giving the Yanks the V-sign, the glad hand, free beer, big smiles, plenty of talk about not being Nazis and hooray for democracy." The Americans were moved by the Aacheners' effusive greetings—returning their smiles and proffering cigarettes and candy bars—but they wasted no time issuing edicts to the civilian population that would become standard rules of conduct in occupied Germany:

A 9 p.m. to 6 a.m. curfew was established, with exceptions for doctors, midwives, nurses and priests; violators could be shot on sight.

Gatherings of more than five people, except in churches, were forbidden.

Any German soldier found in civilian clothing would be shot as a spy.

Newspapers were banned until further notice.

The display of posters and German or Nazi flags was forbidden, as was the playing of German patriotic music.

All schools were to remain closed.

Trips of more than three miles could be made only with special permission.

Fraternization between Americans and Germans was forbidden.

After posting their rules, the occupiers began screening the estimated 10,000 surviving residents of Aachen for men to form a civilian government. Finding the right ones was no easy matter. For one thing, the Americans did not want to put party members into positions of authority—despite a warning from the Bishop of Aachen that "the deeper you go into Germany, the more difficulty you will have in finding non-Nazis." For another, many men were afraid to serve; they feared retribution at the hands of the Werewolves, a guerrilla resistance group made up of Nazi fanatics that was supposed to spring into action in occupied territory.

Nevertheless, the Americans eventually found enough men who had not been Nazis and who were willing to serve. By the end of October, Aachen had a mayor and a 100-man police force working alongside the Occupation forces. The man the Americans installed as mayor was Franz Oppenhoff, a native of the city and a prominent Catholic layman. Oppenhoff had been a lawyer, and among his clients had been the Catholic bishop and several Jewish businessmen. By 1940, these associations had made him a marked man—the Gestapo had labeled his file "Reliability questionable." The district party leader, Eduard Schmeer, went a step further, openly calling Oppenhoff "Public Enemy Number One" and inviting the Gestapo in to search his offices. The police found nothing incriminating, so Schmeer tried to silence Oppenhoff by having him called up for the armed forces; lawyer Oppenhoff managed to keep client Oppenhoff out of the service, but to avoid further trouble he gave up his legal practice and went to work at the local armaments factory.

The Americans discovered Oppenhoff and his family in Eupen, just over the border in Belgium—where they had fled rather than be evacuated eastward—and offered him the mayoral post. Oppenhoff was afraid to take it, telling his wife, "Somewhere or other, there already is a paratrooper assigned to the task of killing me." But his old friend, the Bishop of Aachen, eventually persuaded him to accept. In time, as Oppenhoff had predicted, it would prove to be a fatal decision.

Under the Occupation government, every German official from Oppenhoff down had an American counterpart who had to approve his decisions. The system worked well, and within two months of Aachen's surrender a functioning city was emerging from the rubble. Several grocery stores, bakeries and butcher shops were open. As before, meat, fats and bread were rationed, but vegetables now were readily available. "Money has practically no value," noted one American. "Since there are no stores except food shops, and since prices are controlled, a person cannot spend more than about 20 marks a month, most of it on food."

With their food requirements assured, the Aacheners' most urgent problem was to find suitable shelter. Alone and in teams they worked to repair lightly damaged homes so they could move out of their bunkers and cellars before winter set in.

There were other signs that Aachen was coming back to life. A 500-bed hospital was opened, as was the city's leading bank—which was forced to start from scratch because its records had either been evacuated or destroyed in the fighting. By the end of 1944, tire and textile factories just outside the city were ready to resume production. Aachen's return to a semblance of normal life had allayed any misgivings the city's residents might have harbored about living under the enemy. Indeed, some of them even put up signs announcing proudly: "This house is occupied by a collaborator with the Americans."

From the earliest days of Aachen's occupation, SS chief Heinrich Himmler had been enraged by such collaboration. In early November, he ordered SS General Karl Gutenberger "to educate the population in question by carrying out the death penalty behind enemy lines." Gutenberger, who was SS Police Commander for the Rhineland, was more concerned with the continuing American advance than with individual retribution, and he was inclined to let the matter rest. But around the time of Himmler's decree, he met with his SS superior, General Hans Pruetzmann, who raised the question: "What have you done about Aachen?"

"Aachen?" Gutenberger echoed, puzzled.

"Yes, that swine the Americans have made chief *Bürgermeister*," Pruetzmann persisted.

"What about him?"

"Well, you've got to liquidate him, haven't you?"

That brief exchange set in motion a plan to assassinate Franz Oppenhoff, although it took the embattled SS several months to assemble its death squad. Then, on the night of March 20, 1945, six parachutists dropped from a captured American B-17 to a spot only a few miles from Aachen. The parachutists were Erich Morgenschweiss, a 16-year-old Hit-ler Youth from a mining town just outside Aachen; Ilse Hirsch, a 23-year-old former League of German Girls leader who had once lived in Aachen; three SS enlisted men, two of whom had been border guards in the area; and Herbert Wenzel, an SS lieutenant who commanded the squad.

Five days later, on the evening of Palm Sunday, Oppenhoff's maid, Elisabeth Gillessen, summoned him from the home of a neighbor. Waiting for him were Wenzel and two of his men. "We're German airmen," they told the mayor. "We were shot down near Brussels three days ago. Now we're trying to make our way back to the German lines. What about getting us passes, Herr Bürgermeister?"

"I can't do that," stammered Oppenhoff, who noted that the men were armed. The maid had also spotted the weapons in the half-darkness and was afraid for her employer. But he calmed her down and told her to make sandwiches for the strangers. He then followed her into the kitchen.

The SS men became jittery, suspecting that Oppenhoff had gone to alert the Americans to their presence; but he had not. Now he was returning. They could hear his footsteps. Wenzel pulled his pistol but inexplicably froze and could not fire. One of the other SS men, an Austrian named Leitgeb, grabbed the lieutenant's pistol, cursed him as a "cowardly sow!" and shot Oppenhoff as he emerged from the doorway. As the mayor fell dying, the SS men fled.

Most of the death squad got away. Leitgeb, Oppenhoff's murderer, was killed in a minefield while escaping; Wenzel dropped from sight a few months later and was never seen again. The other members survived and were tried after the War—with young Morgenschweiss as the chief prosecution witness. Ilse Hirsch was acquitted; the other SS men were convicted but received suspended sentences.

With the murder of Oppenhoff, Himmler had gained his

A sign written in German and English and posted by American GIs in Aachen holds up the Führer's promise to ironic commentary. Approximately 75 Allied air raids, followed by weeks of American artillery bombardment, had battered the captured city beyond recognition.

revenge, striking far into what was now enemy territory. Indeed, at the time of the mayor's assassination, roughly 15 per cent of Germany was ruled by the Allies. Much of what remained of Hitler's Third Reich was in ruins, including beautiful Dresden, which Allied bombs had transformed into a charnel house.

On the night of February 13, 1945, in the town of Altenburg, Ilse Heimerdinger Pilger—who earlier had married her dead fiancé in a bizarre wedding ceremony—had settled down with a book, carrying out her self-imposed "Drahtfunk duty" by keeping one ear cocked to the radio for the first indication that enemy planes were approaching. It was 9 o'clock and everyone else in the house was asleep. Ilse turned off the lights and opened the blackout curtain and window to get a breath of fresh air. "It was a lovely, clear night," she later recalled, "and I breathed in deeply, wondering what would happen."

Suddenly the steady ticking of the *Drahtfunk,* an indication that there were no enemy bombers over Germany, stopped. There was a momentary silence. Ilse hurriedly closed the window and pulled back the curtain. Then the radio began to emit the pinging sound that indicated an imminent air raid. An announcer came on to report that a large formation of Allied bombers had just crossed the frontier and was heading in an easterly direction, target as yet unknown. Ilse decided not to wake the others. After a while she dozed off, only to be awakened by a second announcement: "Attention, please! Attention! Large formations of enemy aircraft, course east, heading for Leipzig or Dresden. An air raid on one of those cities is expected."

Ilse switched on the lights. It was 9:30 p.m. What had the announcer said? she asked herself. Leipzig or Dresden? In either case the bombers would pass near Altenburg, only 25 miles southwest of Leipzig and 55 miles west of Dresden. It too might be a target. She decided to awaken the household and get everyone into the cellar. "I banged on all the doors furiously, waking everyone as fast as I could," she said. "We were rushing round the house, turning off lights and opening windows, when the first lot came across."

Ilse and her family were lucky that night. The bombers were heading not for Altenburg, but for Dresden. Because it offered few strategic targets, Dresden had suffered only two light raids in the entire War. The evident immunity of the city had led German authorities to pack it with hundreds of thousands of refugees from the East, and with a large number of British and American POWs who were being marched west away from the advancing Red Army. Now, however, the British and Americans—to convince Soviet dictator Josef Stalin that they were doing everything they could to aid the Russian offensive in the East—had selected the so-called Pearl of Saxony as a bombing objective.

At exactly 10:10 p.m., 244 British bombers appeared over Dresden and began dropping high-explosive and incendiary bombs on the heart of the baroque city. There was virtually no opposition, for the city's flak defenses had been shifted elsewhere after years of disuse. The high explosives shattered windows and staved in the roofs and walls while the incendiaries unleashed a whirlwind of sparks that ignited exposed timbers, curtains and furniture. The British called this lethal combination of bombs the "Hamburg treatment," for they had used the technique on that city nearly two years earlier. The result in Dresden was a storm of fire that robbed the air of oxygen and scorched everything in its path.

In the next 14 hours, two succeeding waves of bombers—including 311 American planes in the final wave—assaulted hapless Dresden, etching every block with flame and destruction. The city's cellars and other shelters were transformed into deadly ovens with temperatures of more than 1,000° F. The streets were no safer. One resident, Bruno Werner, was out walking when he heard a blast and suddenly felt a curtain of heat sweeping over him. A cloud of dust nearly suffocated him. When he finally stopped coughing, he noticed the houses around him "swaying to and fro like blazing scenery on a stage." He worked gradually through the inferno toward the city's popular Grosser Garten, stepping over the dead everywhere; many corpses were so charred that they crunched under his feet. Finally, Werner could go no farther. Shutting his eyes, he leaned against the trunk of a tree that somehow had survived the heat, slid down it and collapsed. "I felt," he said, "like a dead man among thousands of dead."

The park had proved a false refuge from the horror engulfing Dresden. Many of the 200,000 refugees camping there suffocated or were burned to death. Numerous others who sought shelter from the heat in giant water tanks drowned when they could not climb back up their steep sides and out of the deep water.

Bruno Werner, as he sat in the park gasping for breath, saw a nearby hospital for blind soldiers and amputees go up in flames. "When the fire started," related Werner, "they let themselves drop out of the windows of the burning structure." Those who landed safely still had to clear a high iron fence for which they had no key. Eventually, Werner recalled, "they built human pyramids. Whoever reached the top let himself fall to the other side of the high fence. Men in striped smocks hopped bare-footed in the hissing embers, supporting themselves with crutches, spades and bars, and they limped or rolled, screaming and in flames. The air grew thinner and the striped ones fell unconscious in the wet, smoldering leaves." Despite his horror, Werner remembered the fire as "a gorgeous spectacle, glittering in violet, lemon-yellow, emerald-green and raspberry-red colors and filled with whimpers and screams, roaring and howling. Outside the fence stood women in smoldering skirts trying to catch those who hurled themselves from the top."

The macabre pyrotechnics that Werner—and others all over Dresden—witnessed were vignettes in a night filled with other-worldly horrors. A fire engine that had been on its way to the soldiers' hospital shuddered to a halt nearby. The engine was still running, but the firemen had suffocated from lack of oxygen. Their uniforms crumbled in the baking air, said Werner, and they sat "naked on their seats, lined up against the metal ladder, with straps around their brown bodies and helmets on their yellow skulls."

In the Lindenauplatz, a square near the city's central railway, rescue workers later found hundreds of corpses similarly denuded by the intense heat of the firestorm. Near the entrance to a streetcar shelter, noted one worker, "was a woman of about 30, completely naked, lying face down on a fur coat. A few yards farther on lay two young boys of about eight and 10 clinging tightly to each other; their faces were buried in the ground. They too were stark naked; their legs were stiff and twisted in the air."

Inside the station, the carnage was particularly gruesome; General Erich Hampe, Germany's chief of emergency rail repair and a veteran of many raids, declared it the worst he had seen. Several thousand refugees from the East had taken shelter in the station's vaulted basement, unaware that there were neither ventilation shafts nor blastproof doors to protect them. When they tried to escape, they found the passageways clogged with baggage.

"Only one thing saved me," said a woman who had just arrived from Silesia with her two infants. "I pushed through into a boiler room underneath one of the platforms. In the thin ceiling was a hole made by a dud incendiary. Through this hole we were able to get sufficient air to breathe now and then. Everyone seemed to be leaning against us. Several hours passed. Then I heard someone shouting, and an Army officer helped me out through a long passage. We passed through the basement; there were several thousand people there, all lying very still."

Many more refugees were caught in the station waiting room. Some of them had been there for several days, hoping to catch a westbound train, and had refused to move for what they thought would be Dresden's 172nd false alarm of the War. When the bombs struck the station, the refugees perished, packed together like so many sardines. "There must have been a children's train at the station," recalled the Silesian mother. "More and more dead children were stacked up, in layers, on top of one another, and covered with blankets. I took one of those blankets for my babies, who were not dead, but alive and terribly cold."

Stacked bodies from the fire bombing of Dresden smolder atop a pyre made of railroad track. To prevent the spread of disease, thousands of those killed in the February 1945 raids were cremated where they had fallen.

A Dresden landmark, the city's Frauenkirche (right) stands before the Allied bombers struck—and after its 300-foot dome had collapsed into rubble. At first, the 18th Century cathedral appeared to have survived the raid. Then spontaneous combustion, induced by oven-high temperatures, ignited the Luftwaffe celluloid film archives stored in the church basement. The resulting explosive fire brought down what the bombers could not.

On the morning of February 14, a pall of smoke from continuing fires hung over the city and its dazed inhabitants. To Hans Köhler, aged 14, a Hitler Youth assigned to the Fire Department, it seemed as though his familiar world had been turned upside down. As he walked toward the Old Town—the center of Dresden and the site of some of its greatest architecture—young Hans was astonished to see a man loyally scrubbing the sarcastic slogan, ''Thank you, dear Führer,'' from a charred sidewalk where someone had painted it after the raid. Farther on, he saw soldiers shoot at men who were gathering cigarettes from the street near a burned-out tobacco factory; and he passed an apartment building where someone, fearing the worst in advance of the raid, had placed a sign: ''We are alive; get us out.'' The sign spurred rescuers trying to break into the basement, but they were turned back by the overwhelming heat.

Few rescue attempts were successful. ''We were lucky to find here and there one or two surviving,'' said one worker. Mostly he found corpses, ''shriveled in the intense heat to about three feet long.''

When Hans Köhler reached the Old Town he found it in ruins. The Opera House—where Wagner's *Tannhäuser* and *Rienzi* had received their premieres almost a century earlier—had been reduced to a smoldering shell; the Zwinger, a palatial old museum housing priceless collections, also had been destroyed.

Already the living had set about the grisly task of identifying and burying the dead. The workers—among them Allied prisoners of war and women from the Labor Service and the Auxiliary War Service—searched the bodies for some item of identity: papers or clothing samples or wedding rings that might bear an inscription. In this ghoulish task, the young women proved as tough as the men, wading into basements and cellars to drag out the corpses. To one group of women fell the poignant duty of identifying 90 of their friends, who had suffocated in the basement of a youth hostel. ''The girls sat there as though stopped in the middle of a conversation,'' said the leader of a squad that broke through to the hostel basement. ''They looked so natural that it was hard to believe they were indeed not alive.''

The authorities never were able to determine the exact

number of people killed in Dresden, whose normal population had been 630,000. An accurate count was impossible because of the large number of refugees passing through the city, and because many bodies were blown to bits or were piled indiscriminately in the streets where they had fallen and were set alight in mass funeral pyres. Propaganda Minister Goebbels, attempting to instill a desire for revenge in the German people, claimed that the final death toll "will exceed 250,000." A later German estimate put the figure at close to 135,000.

As Dresden buried its dead, Albert Speer was trying to prevent Hitler from fulfilling a pledge that, if carried out, would bring further ruin to what remained of Germany. The previous September, Hitler had vowed to scorch the earth as the Allies advanced. "Not a German stalk of wheat is to feed the enemy, not a German mouth to give him information, not a German hand to offer him help," declared an editorial, dictated by Hitler, in the party newspaper. "He is to find every footbridge destroyed, every road blocked—nothing but death, annihilation and hatred will greet him." At the time, Speer had managed to forestall the scorched-earth policy by convincing Hitler that it would be foolish to demolish factories, roads and bridges in territory that would soon be reconquered. But as the Allies advanced deeper and deeper into Germany, the Führer once more became obsessed with destroying what was left of the home front in order to deny it to the enemy. Speer decided that this time he would need more than persuasion to stop Hitler.

In early February, Friedrich Lüschen, head of the German electrical industry, visited Speer in the apartment he kept at his Ministry on Berlin's Pariser Platz. "Are you aware," he asked Speer, "of the passage from Hitler's *Mein Kampf* that is most often quoted by the public nowadays?" Lüschen handed Speer a slip of paper that read: "The task of diplomacy is to ensure that a nation does not go heroically to its destruction but is practically preserved. Every way that leads to this end is expedient and a failure to follow it must be called criminal neglect of duty." Lüschen then handed Speer a second quotation from *Mein Kampf*: "If a racial entity is being led toward its doom by means of governmental power, then the rebellion of every single member of such a *Volk* is not only a right but a duty."

Lüschen left without another word, leaving his quotations with Speer. "Here was Hitler himself saying what I had been trying to get across these past months," Speer thought. "Only one conclusion remained to be drawn: Hitler himself—measured by the standards of his own political program—was deliberately committing high treason against his own people, who had made great sacrifices for his cause, and to whom he owed everything." That night, Speer wrote, "I came to the decision to eliminate Hitler."

On walks through the gardens of the Reich Chancellery, Hitler's headquarters, Speer had noticed that the ventilation shaft for Hitler's bunker was readily accessible at ground level and was covered only by a thin grating. It would be a simple matter, he believed, to drop poison gas down the shaft. If he were lucky, he might be able to eliminate not only Hitler, but Bormann, Goebbels and Robert Ley "during one of their nocturnal chats." Speer arranged to get a canister of poison gas from a subordinate who headed munitions production—a man he had once saved from the Gestapo and who he was sure would not betray him.

At the same time, Speer mentioned to the Chancellery's

Antitank weapons strapped to their handlebars and rifles slung across their backs, Hitler Youths ride through the ruin of a camoflaged street in Frankfurt an der Oder in February of 1945. Such youngsters were Hitler's last pool of manpower for the defense of the homeland.

chief engineer, a man named Henschel, that the bunker's air filters needed changing; Hitler, he said, had been complaining about bad air in the bunker. The hint that the Führer was unhappy was all it took. "Quicker than I could possibly act," Speer recalled, "Henschel removed the filtering system, so that the bunker was without protection."

But soon after, when Speer invented a pretext to inspect the ventilation shaft, he found armed SS guards, searchlights, and a 10-foot-high chimney in place of the ground-level shaft. Speer's first thought was that his plan had been discovered. Actually, the construction of the chimney at that time was pure coincidence. Hitler, who had been temporarily blinded by gas in World War I, did in fact fear a gas attack and had ordered the chimney installed—but he had no idea Speer had been planning to kill him in that way.

Speer gave up his plan. "I no longer considered it my mission to eliminate Hitler," he later wrote, "but to frustrate his orders for destruction." On an inspection trip to Silesia in mid-February, Speer convinced General Gotthard Heinrici, commander of an army group massed along the Oder River, that railroads in the region should not be destroyed, as Hitler had ordered, since they would be needed after the War to deliver coal to southeastern Germany. Likewise in early March he persuaded Field Marshal Walther Model to leave bridges and railroad lines intact in the industrial Ruhr. And he arranged for General Heinz Guderian, head of operations in the East, to issue a decree forbidding his subordinates to carry out any demolition that would "hinder the supplying of our own population."

When Guderian tried to persuade General Alfred Jodl, chief of Germany's operations in the West, to issue a similar decree, Jodl refused and referred the matter to Field Marshal Wilhelm Keitel, Chief of Staff of the Armed Forces. Keitel informed Hitler of the decree, with predictable results: Hitler raved and ranted and reiterated his instructions for scorched earth everywhere. Desperate, Speer decided to appeal directly to Hitler one last time. In mid-March, he prepared a 22-page memorandum detailing "with certainty, the final collapse of the German economy" within four to eight weeks. "No one," he wrote, "has the right to take the viewpoint that the fate of the German people is tied to his personal fate. At this stage of the War, it makes no sense for us to undertake demolitions that may strike at the very life of the nation."

Up to that point, Speer had argued that factories had to be left intact so they could be returned to operation after the reconquest. Now, he was both attacking Hitler and declaring that Germany's industrial and material wealth had to be preserved "even if a reconquest does not seem possible."

Speer gave his memorandum to Hitler on the evening of March 18, shortly after the Führer had adjourned his daily situation meeting with military and civilian aides. During that meeting, Hitler had ordered the evacuation of all civilians who were in the path of the American Army by whatever means necessary—the same kind of order that he had issued when Aachen was threatened. When one of his generals told him that no trains were available to transport the evacuees, Hitler had snapped, "Let them walk. We no longer can concern ourselves with the population." Clearly, the Führer was in a foul mood, and Speer trembled inwardly as he handed Hitler a document that "dryly set forth the collapse of his entire mission."

Hitler took the memorandum without a word and dismissed Speer. A short time later, he summoned Speer to his study. "You will receive a written reply to your memorandum," he said icily. He paused a moment, then continued. "If the War is lost, the people will be lost also. It is not necessary to worry about what the German people will need for elemental survival. On the contrary, it is best for us to destroy even these things. For the nation has proved to be the weaker. In any case, only those who are inferior will remain after the struggle, for the good already have been killed." With that, Hitler dismissed Speer.

Though the Führer would remain in his Berlin bunker almost to the War's bitter end, he had, with that harsh pronouncement, deserted the German people once and for all.

FLIGHT FROM THE RUSSIANS

Caught in a waking nightmare, a German family flees through a forest in eastern Germany in the spring of 1945, one step ahead of the advancing Red Army.

A FLOOD TIDE OF REFUGEES

The impending collapse of their nation left the German people feeling bitter, betrayed and—at least in the east—terrified. The Russians, bent on revenge, were swarming over their land; as the Red Army advanced, nearly half of the 15 million Germans in the eastern provinces of the Reich fled for their lives.

For a few high officials, there were private cars and planes to escape in. Others fled by bus or train—though toward the end, the few trains available were packed so tight that frequent checks were made to throw off the dead and make room inside for those riding the roofs. Panic and confusion prevailed: In one instance, flatcars carrying 142 children were separated from a train and forgotten for days. When they were found, all the children had frozen to death.

Most refugees made their way west by wagon and sleigh or on foot in massive caravans numbering as many as 30,000 people, the majority of them women and children. Once on the road, they were shelled and strafed by Russian tanks and planes. Cold, fatigue and hunger were equally unrelenting enemies. Mothers risked frostbite to breast-feed their babies in subzero weather. One woman took the shoes off a dead refugee only to discover that the frozen flesh had peeled off with them. Ravenous cart horses gnawed at their leather rigs or starved to death in harness; their owners, not much better off, carved chunks of meat from the horses' flanks and left the carcasses to rot in roadside ditches.

The Germans who stayed behind paid dearly. In village after village the men were slaughtered or deported to the Soviet Union as slave labor. Women and girls—including some 12 years old or younger—were raped and raped again. Cities and farms alike were plundered and burned.

Even those who evaded the Red Army were not always safe. Thousands perished at sea en route to ports in northwest Europe. Families fleeing overland to cities like Dresden arrived just in time to be hammered by the last waves of Allied bombers. And for the survivors, peace brought a final trial: months, sometimes years, in the purgatory of refugee camps.

German officers inspect the bodies of villagers shot by Red Army troops in October of 1944. News of such atrocities set off an exodus to the west.

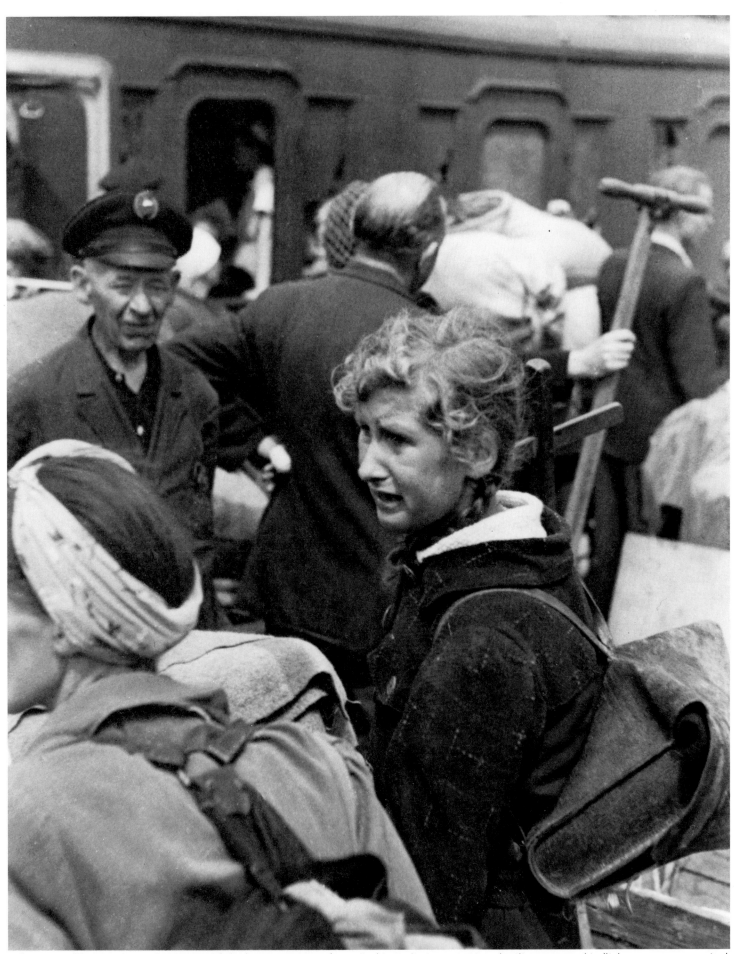

Refugee Angelika Mewes searches in anguish for her parents upon her arrival in Berlin in 1945. Many families, separated in flight, were never reunited.

EARLY CARAVANS TO SAFETY

Refugees who got away early or lived farthest west had a fairly easy trek. Many caravans in the autumn of 1944 had official leaders and military escorts to smooth their way. Fuel was still available, so farmers could drive to safety with their belongings. And the weather was still mild.

Yet even an unhurried flight was emotionally painful. Farms were abandoned by people who had never been more than a few miles from home—and whose families had lived in one region for centuries. In industrial Silesia, families were split up; the women and children left and the men stayed behind to work the coal mines and factories. Many who fled early would have to retreat again—when the havens they had reached were themselves overrun.

With the assistance of Wehrmacht troopers, German refugees heading westward drive their farm wagons and livestock across a shallow country stream.

Bundled onto a truck, Silesian women—including a nun—smile their good-bys to Breslau in late 1944.

Preparing to travel heavy, Silesians load a double wagon with possessions for the journey west.

A FIRST TASTE OF HORROR

The Red Army first entered German territory in October of 1944. Although the Russians were temporarily driven out again, they stayed long enough to occupy a few villages—and to confirm the worst fears of the German nation.

Husbands and fathers, sons and brothers were made to hold lamps and watch while whole squads of soldiers violated their women. If the men resisted they were shot, or castrated and then shot. Women who resisted too strongly were knifed and disemboweled. Officers pulled rank to rape the prettiest young women. The author Alexander Solzhenitsyn, then a captain in the Red Army, sorrowfully wrote: "Whoever still a virgin, soon to become a woman; the women soon to become corpses. Eyes bloody, already glazed over, pleading: 'Kill me, soldier.'"

Villagers who fled in sleighs over the early snow as the Russians approached were sometimes chased in sleighs with Soviet machine guns mounted on them. German militiamen were doused in gasoline and set aflame. Women were nailed naked to barn doors; babies with their heads bashed in littered the floors of ravaged homes. Some Germans survived this first bitter taste of invasion with the help of Polish servants, who disguised them to pass as Poles. But such fortunate ones were few.

Reports of the atrocities flew to every corner of the Reich. Hitler exploited the accounts to steel his troops. But for civilians in the line of advance, they offered compelling reason to run for their lives and not look back.

Fire and panic herald the arrival of Red Army guns on the outskirts of Breslau as civilians, some of their wagon horses already killed by the shelling, hurry to evacuate ahead of the Russians. Soviet troops were urged on by propaganda leaflets proclaiming: "The hour of revenge has struck!"

Wrapped in blankets and furs, refugees drag their sleds down a snow-clogged path. Caravans sometimes trudged just two or three miles a day, and were easily overtaken by the motorized Russians.

DEATH ON A FROZEN ROAD

Not everyone who ran for safety made it. The Russians overtook and obliterated many caravans whose members had trusted too long in optimistic Nazi propaganda or had been held up on the road—often by the influx of entire villages hurrying to join them in flight.

Once under way, the refugees found the weather a tormenter as brutal as the Red Army. The winter of 1944-1945 proved to be one of the worst in memory; a cutting east wind blew relentlessly, and temperatures stayed below zero for weeks at a time. Horses failed and carts broke down on the icy roads. Ditches were strewn with abandoned belongings—and with dead babies, put there by mothers anxious to protect the bodies from being run over.

When not being attacked, the wagon trains were eerily quiet, as though everyone was waiting for death, or a miracle. "Some women tried to sit down on their sleds for a rest," one survivor recalled, "but the cold drove them on, all except those who simply stayed there and perhaps froze to death with their children."

Having arrived too late to help, German soldiers survey the damage sustained by a civilian

wagon train that had been machine-gunned by the Russians; soldiers atop the Tiger tank in the distance scan the horizon for any trace of the attackers.

Refugees with wagons and bicycles—and even a house on wheels—cross the frozen Frisches Haff. Small clusters moved at intervals to reduce the strain on the ice.

DESPERATE CROSSING OVER THIN ICE

By late January, 1945, the Red Army had severed all eastern rail links with Berlin; the wagon routes too had been cut in many places. So Germans in the north sought to escape by sea from ports in East Prussia. To reach open water, many of them had to traverse a daunting obstacle: the Frisches Haff, a frozen lagoon that separated the mainland from the Baltic.

The five-mile crossing took as long as 12 hours on the open ice. One wagon of every three that started across broke down or was abandoned; many sank through the ice, leaving mothers desperately searching the edges for signs of their children. Soviet air attacks were doubly destructive. Even if the bombs missed, the craters they blew open could suck in rows of wagons.

As winter neared its end, the lagoon began to thaw. The most determined refugees waded through a foot of water, testing the ice with each timorous step. Thousands more waited on the shore, praying for what they had earlier dreaded—cold weather, to refreeze the lagoon.

Leaving their carts behind, refugees walk to the melting ice's edge to reach ships that took them the rest of the way across the lagoon.

STANDING ROOM ONLY AT BALTIC PORTS

In all, some 500,000 refugees made the perilous crossing to reach—and clog—such Baltic ports as Danzig and Gdynia. Pillau swelled from 5,000 to 50,000 residents almost overnight. As they waited for ships to carry them farther west, the refugees slept where they could—in warehouses, doorways, deserted streetcars—and ate at soup kitchens that were provisioned by the slaughter of stray cattle.

At first only the well-to-do could afford passage, for captains charged high prices. Then only women and children were taken—a priority that led to some bizarre actions. Men tried to bluff their way on dressed as women. Small children, a sure pass to boarding, were pitched from deck to dock so that the childless could get on

Wagons, bicycles and a tethered goat remain at the side of the dock in a Baltic port, left behind because there was no room for them on the refugee ships.

too. Some youngsters fell in and drowned.

Packed with humanity, the ships offered warmth many of the refugees had not felt in weeks. But at sea they were targets for Russian submarines and even for misguided German warships. About 25,000 refugees drowned in the Baltic—nearly 7,000 of them on one torpedoed ship, the *Goya*, which sank in four minutes.

Priority passengers—mothers, children and babies in carriages—crowd aboard a ship at Pillau on the Baltic Sea in the spring of 1945. The rescue ships also evacuated thousands of wounded German soldiers.

Thankful for standing room, refugees cram every available inch of space on a German rescue vessel and overflow into a lifeboat suspended in its davits. The voyage to safety required three to four days.

FOR THE FORTUNATE, DELIVERANCE BY SEA

Never had there been a sealift like it. Cruise ships, whalers, barges, tankers, tugs and the remnants of the German Navy—790 vessels in all—carried more than two million refugees to ports in northwest Germany and German-occupied Denmark.

Some ships were in such disrepair that they had to be towed into port. (One transport vessel, unseaworthy from the start, was towed the whole way from Danzig to Copenhagen.) Even after Germany surrendered the evacuation went on, as ships limping westward refused to put into the nearest ports for fear that they might come under Soviet control.

All the while, the millions who had fled overland continued to pour into western cities—free, now, from the ravages of Allied bombing. All of them had hopes—but no real chance—of returning home. Instead, for those who journeyed far enough, peace brought internment and, eventually, a fresh start in the west.

The passenger ship Pretoria, her funnels marked with red crosses, arrives at Copenhagen on April 20, 1945, with a full load of refugees. Though many people died at sea, others were born there—and often were named for the ships that had rescued them.

BIBLIOGRAPHY

Andreas-Friedrich, Ruth, *Berlin Underground*. Transl. by Barrows Mussey. Henry Holt and Company, 1947.

Bailey, Ronald H., and the Editors of Time-Life Books, *The Air War in Europe* (World War II series). Time-Life Books Inc., 1979.

Baker, Leonard, *Days of Sorrow and Pain: Leo Baeck and the Berlin Jews*. London: Oxford University Press, 1978.

Barker, Ralph, and the Editors of Time-Life Books, *The RAF at War* (The Epic of Flight series). Time-Life Books Inc., 1981.

Bielenberg, Christabel, *The Past Is Myself*. London: Chatto & Windus, 1968.

Blondes, Georges, *Death of Hitler's Germany*. Macmillan, 1954.

Boberach, Heinz, ed., *Meldungen aus dem Reich*. Neuwied, Federal Republic of Germany: Hermann Luchterhand Verlag, 1965.

Boehm, Eric H., *We Survived: Fourteen Histories of the Hidden and Hunted of Nazi Germany*. Clio Press, 1966.

Bullock, Alan, *Hitler*. Harper & Row, 1962.

Burden, Hamilton T., *The Nuremberg Party Rallies: 1923-1939*. Frederick A. Praeger, 1967.

"Covering Air-Raid Protection and Allied Subjects in Germany." United States Strategic Bombing Survey, Civilian Defense Division, October 29, 1945.

Craig, Gordon A., *Germany, 1866-1945*. London: Oxford University Press, 1978.

Dietrich, Otto, *Hitler*. Transl. by Richard and Clara Winston. Henry Regnery Company, 1955.

Dulles, Allen Welsh, *Germany's Underground*. Greenwood Press, 1947.

"The Effect of Bombing on Health and Medical Care in Germany." The United States Strategic Bombing Survey, Morale Division, October 30, 1945.

Fest, Joachim C.:
The Face of the Third Reich. Transl. by Michael Bullock. Pantheon Books, 1970.
Hitler. Transl. by Richard and Clara Winston. Vintage Books, 1973.

Flannery, Harry W., *Assignment to Berlin*. Alfred A. Knopf, 1942.

Flower, Desmond, and James Reeves, *The Taste of Courage: The War, 1939-1945*. Harper & Row, Publishers, 1960.

Franks, Ivan B., "German Civil Defense." Allied Forces, Supreme Headquarters, Air Defense Division, May 1955.

Frischauer, Willi, *The Rise and Fall of Hermann Goering*. The Riverside Press, 1951.

Gersdorff, Ursula von, *Frauen im Kriegsdienst*. Stuttgart: Deutsche Verlags-Anstalt, 1969.

Goldston, Robert, *The Life and Death of Nazi Germany*. The Bobbs-Merrill Company, 1967.

Gotto, Klaus, and Konrad Repgen, eds., *Kirche, Katholiken und Nationalsozialismus*. Mainz, Federal Republic of Germany: Matthias-Grünewald-Verlag, 1980.

Grebling, Helga, *Der Nationalsozialismus*. Munich: Isar Verlag, 1959.

"Grosz/Heartfield: The Artist as Social Critic." University Gallery, University of Minnesota, 1980.

Grunberger, Richard, *The 12-Year Reich: A Social History of Nazi Germany 1933-1945*. Holt, Rinehart and Winston, 1971.

Grunfeld, Frederick V., *The Hitler File: A Social History of Germany and the Nazis 1918-1945*. Random House, 1974.

Hampe, Erich, *Der Zivile Luftschutz im Zweiten Weltkrieg*. Frankfurt am Main, Federal Republic of Germany: Bernard & Graefe Verlag für Wehrwesen, 1963.

Hanser, Richard, *A Noble Treason: The Revolt of the Munich Students against Hitler*. G. P. Putnam's Sons, 1979.

Hastings, Max, *Bomber Command*. The Dial Press, 1979.

Herzstein, Robert Edwin, *The War That Hitler Won*. G. P. Putnam's Sons, 1978.

Herzstein, Robert Edwin, and the Editors of Time-Life Books, *The Nazis* (World War II series). Time-Life Books Inc., 1980.

Hilberg, Raul, *The Destruction of the European Jews*. Octagon Books, 1978.

Hitler, Adolf, *Mein Kampf*. Transl. by Dr. Alvin Johnson. Reynal & Hitchcock, 1939.

Hitler-Jugend. Hamburg, Federal Republic of Germany: Verlag für Geschichtliche Documentation, no date.

Hogg, Ian V., *Anti-Aircraft: A History of Air Defense*. London: MacDonald and Jane's, 1978.

Höhne, Heinz, *The Order of the Death's Head*. Transl. by Richard Barry. Ballantine Books, 1969.

Homze, Edward L., *Foreign Labor in Nazi Germany*. Princeton University Press, 1967.

Horstmann, Frederick, *Friedrich von Bodelschwingh*. Bielefeld, Federal Republic of Germany: Druck Robert Bechauf, 1972.

Hubmann, Hanns, *Augenzeuge: 1933-1945*. Berlin, Munich: F. A. Herbig Verlagsbuchhandlung, 1980.

Hull, David Stewart, *Film in the Third Reich*. Simon and Schuster, 1969.

Irving, David, *The Destruction of Dresden*. Holt, Rinehart and Winston, 1963.

Kahn, David, *Hitler's Spies: German Military Intelligence in World War II*. Macmillan Publishing Co., Inc., 1978.

Kardorff, Ursula von, *Diary of a Nightmare: Berlin 1942-1945*. Transl. by Ewan Butler. The John Day Company, 1965.

Kempowski, Walter:
Haben Sie Hitler Gesehen? Hamburg: Albrecht Knaus, 1973.
Tadellöser & Wolff. Hamburg: Albrecht Knaus, 1975.

Knauth, Barbara, Christina and Sybilla, "The Chimneys of Leipzig: Three American Girls Tell the Story of How Germany's Third Largest City Was Destroyed." *Life*, May 15, 1944.

Knef, Hildegard, *The Gift Horse*. Transl. by David Anthony Palastanga. McGraw-Hill Book Company, 1971.

Koch, Horst-Adalbert, *Flak: Die Geschichte der Deutschen Flakartillerie*. Bad-Neuheim, Federal Republic of Germany: Verlag Hans-Henning Podzun, 1954.

Koch, H. W., *The Hitler Youth: Origins and Development 1922-1945*. London: MacDonald and Jane's, 1975.

Kogon, Edith, *The Theory and Practice of Hell: The German Concentration Camps and the System behind Them*. Transl. by Heinz Norden. Berkley Publishing Corporation, 1960.

König, Joel, *David*. Frankfurt am Main, Federal Republic of Germany: Fischer Taschenbuch Verlag, 1967.

Laqueur, Walter Z., *Young Germany: A History of the German Youth Movement*. Basic Books Publishing Co., Inc., 1962.

Leiser, Erwin, *Nazi Cinema*. Transl. by Gertrud Mander and David Wilson. Macmillan, 1974.

McKee, Ilse, *Tomorrow the World*. London: J. M. Dent & Sons, 1960.

Manvell, Roger, and Heinrich Fraenkel, *The German Cinema*. Frederick A. Praeger, 1971.

Maschmann, Melita, *Account Rendered*. Transl. by Geoffrey Steichan, Abelard Schuman, 1964.

Mertens, Eberhard, ed., *Filmprogramme: Ein Querschnitt durch das Deutsche Filmschaffen:*
Vol. 1: *1930-1939*. Hildesheim, Federal Republic of Germany: Olms Presse, 1977.
Vol. 2: *1940-1945*. Hildesheim, Federal Republic of Germany: Olms Presse, 1977.

Middlebrook, Martin, *The Nuremberg Raid: 30-31 March 1944*. William Morrow & Company, Inc., 1973.

Mosse, George L., *Nazi Culture Intellectual, Cultural and Social Life in the Third Reich*. Transl. by Salvator Attanasio and others. Grosset & Dunlap, 1966.

The Nazi Primer. Transl. by Harwood L. Childs. Harper & Brothers Publishers, 1938.

Niemöller, Martin:
From U-boat to Pulpit. Willett, Clark & Company, 1937.
The Gestapo Defied. William Hodge & Company, Ltd., 1941.

Noakes, Jeremy, and Geoffrey Pridham, *Documents on Nazism, 1919-1945*. The Viking Press, 1974.

Nosbüsch, Johannes, *Bis zum Bitteren Ende: Der Zweite Weltkreig im Kreis Bitburg-Prüm*. Bitburg-Prüm, Federal Republic of Germany: Kreisverwaltung Bitburg-Prüm, no date.

Padover, Saul K., *Experiment in Germany*. Duell, Sloan and Pearce, 1946.

Paul, Wolfgang, *Der Heimatkrieg: 1939 bis 1945*. Esslingen am Neckar, Federal Republic of Germany: Bechtle, 1980.

Petley, Julian, *Capital and Culture: German Cinema 1933-1945*. London: British Film Institute, 1979.

Prittie, Terence, *Germans against Hitler*. Little, Brown & Company, 1964.

Richards, Denis, *Royal Air Force 1939-1945*, Vol. 1, *The Fight at Odds*. London: Her Majesty's Stationery Office, 1974.

Richards, Denis, and Hilary St. George Saunders, *Royal Air Force 1939-1945*, Vol. 2, *The Fight Avails*. London: Her Majesty's Stationery Office, 1975.

Roh, Franz, *Entartete Kunst*. Hanover, Federal Republic of Germany: Fackelträger-Verlag, no date.

Rumpf, Hans, *The Bombing of Germany*. Transl. by Edward Fitzgerald. London: White Lion Publishers Limited, 1963:

Rupp, Leila J., *Mobilizing Women for War: German and American Propaganda, 1939-1945*. Princeton University Press, 1978.

"Mit dem Säbel gegen Deutsche Panzer." *Bild am Sonntag*, Hamburg, September 9, 1979.

Saunders, Hilary St. George, *Royal Air Force 1939-1945*, Vol. 3, *The Fight is Won*. London: Her Majesty's Stationery Office, 1975.

Schaeffer, L., "Camouflage: German Experience in the Camouflage of Rear-Area Civil Installations." Transl. by P. W. Luetzkendorf. Koenigstein, Federal Republic of Germany: Historical Division, European Command, Project #28, September 27, 1950.

Schmidt-Luchs, Hugo and Werner, *Hamburg: Phönix aus der Asche*. Hamburg: Harry V. Hofmann Verlag, 1979.

Schoenbaum, David, *Hitler's Social Revolution: Class and Status in Nazi Germany, 1933-1939*. Doubleday & Company, Inc., 1966.

Scholl, Inge, *Students against Tyranny*. Transl. by Arthur R. Schultz. Wesleyan University Press, 1952.

Schütz, W. W., and B. De Seven, *German Home Front*. London: Victor Gollancz, 1943.

"Die Schwarze Madonna Hat Gesagt: Du Darfst Töten!" *Bild am Sonntag*, Hamburg, September 23, 1979.

Seiler, Harald, *Flak an Rhein und Ruhr*. Münster, Federal Republic of Germany: Wehrbetreuung, 1942.

Senger, Valentin, *No. 12 Kaiserhofstrasse*. Transl. by Ralph Manheim. E. P. Dutton, 1980.

Seydewitz, Max, *Civil Life in Wartime Germany: The Story of the Home Front*. The Viking Press, 1945.

Shirer, William L.:
Berlin Diary: The Journal of a Foreign Correspondent, 1934-1941. Alfred A. Knopf, 1941.
The Rise and Fall of the Third Reich. Simon and Schuster, 1960.

Smith, Howard K., *Last Train from Berlin*. Popular Library, 1942.

Solzhenitsyn, Alexander, *Prussian Nights: A Poem*. Farrar, Straus and Giroux, 1977.

Speer, Albert, *Inside the Third Reich*. Transl. by Richard and Clara Winston. Avon, 1970.

Stachura, Peter D., *Nazi Youth in the Weimar Republic*. Clio Books, 1975.

Steinert, Marlis G., *Hitler's War and the Germans: Public Mood and Attitude During the Second World War*. Ed. and transl. by Thomas E. J. DeWitt. Ohio University Press, 1977.

Taylor, Eric, *1000 Bomber auf Köln: Operation Millenium 1942*. Düsseldorf, Federal Republic of Germany: Droste Verlag, 1979.

Taylor, Richard, *Film Propaganda: Soviet Russia and Nazi Germany*. Barnes & Noble Books, 1979.

Toland, John, *The Last 100 Days*. Random House, 1966.

Unikower, Inge, *Suche nach dem Gelobten Land*. Berlin: Verlag der Nation, 1978.

Webster, Sir Charles, and Noble Frankland, *The Strategic Air Offensive against Germany 1939-1945*, Vol. 4. London: Her Majesty's Stationery Office, 1961.

Werstein, Irving, *The Battle of Aachen*. Thomas Y. Crowell Company, 1962.

Whiting, Charles:
    Bloody Aachen. Stein and Day, 1976.
    Hitler's Werewolves, The Story of the Nazi Resistance Movement, 1944-1945. Stein and Day, 1972.

Whiting, Charles, and Friedrich Gehendges, *Jener September*. Düsseldorf, Federal Republic of Germany: Droste Verlag, 1979.

Wolff-Monckeberg, Mathilde, *On the Other Side: To My Children, from Germany, 1940-1945*. Ed. and transl. by Ruth Evans. Mayflower Books, 1979.

Wykes, Alan, *The Nuremberg Rallies*. Ballantine, 1970.

Ziemke, Earl F., *The U.S. Army in the Occupation of Germany: 1944-1946*. Center of Military History, United States Army, 1975.

PICTURE CREDITS

Credits from left to right are separated by semicolons, from top to bottom by dashes.

ACKNOWLEDGMENTS

For help given in the preparation of this book, the editors wish to express their gratitude to Inge Aicher-Scholl, Rotis/Leutkirch, Federal Republic of Germany; Ed Baines, United States Army Center for Military History, Washington, D.C.; Joergen H. Barfod, Director, The Museum for Denmark's Fight for Freedom 1940-1945, Copenhagen; Erich Behnke, Cologne; Véronique Blum, Chief Curator, Musée des Deux Guerres Mondiales, Paris; Ralf Bollhorn, Hauptfeuerwache, Hamburg; Hans Brunswig, Hamburg; Wolfgang Busch, Ahrensburg, Federal Republic of Germany; Clinton B. Conger, McLean, Virginia; Cécile Coutin, Curator, Musée des Deux Guerres Mondiales, Paris; Brigitte Emmer, Institut für Zeitgeschichte, Munich; Lotte Fischer, Cologne; Vilma Frielingsdorf, Berlin (West); Mary Lou Gjernes, United States Army Center for Military History, Washington, D.C.; Micky Glässge, Deutsches Institut für Filmkunde, Wiesbaden, Federal Republic of Germany; Barbara Glavert-Hesse, von Bodel-Schwinghsche Anstalten, Bielefeld; L. Fritz Gruber, Stadtarchiv, Cologne; Werner Haupt, Bibliothek für Zeitgeschichte, Stuttgart; Gertrude Heartfield, Berlin, DDR; E. C. Hine, Department of Photographs, Imperial War Museum, London; Heinrich Hoffmann, Hamburg; Freye Jeschke, Librarian, Goethe House, New York; Walter Kempowski, Nartum/Bremen, Federal Republic of Germany; Heidi Klein, Bildarchiv Preussischer Kulturbesitz, Berlin (West); Dr. Roland Klemig, Bildarchiv Preussischer Kulturbesitz, Berlin (West); Rosemarie Klipp, Bonn; Dieter Knippschild, Dortmund, Federal Republic of Germany; Roy Koch, Bonn; Walter Kuchta, Cologne; Doris Leinekugel, Inter Nationes, Bonn; Gustav Luntowski, Stadtarchiv, Dortmund, Federal Republic of Germany; Peter Magdovski, Stiftung Deutsche Kinemathek, Berlin (West); Bjarne Maurer, Research Fellow, The Museum of Denmark's Fight for Freedom 1940-1945, Copenhagen; Françoise Mercier, Institut d'Histoire du Temps Présent, Paris; Dr. Sybil Milton, Chief Archivist, Leo Baeck Institute, New York; Timothy Mulligan, Department of Modern Military History, National Archives, Washington, D.C.; Meinrad Nilges, Bundesarchiv, Koblenz; Herbert Orstein, Zentralbibliothek der Bundeswehr, Düsseldorf; Dee Pattee, Munich; George A. Peterson, Springfield, Virginia; Marco Pincus, ABC Antiquariat, Zurich; Hannes Quaschinsky, ADN-Zentralbild, Berlin, DDR; Helmut Regel, Bundesarchiv, Koblenz; Dr. Jürgen Rohwer, Stuttgart; Gerd Sachsse, Bonn; Gerd Sander, Silver Spring, Maryland; Gunther Sander, Rottach-Egern, Federal Republic of Germany; P. F. Sargeant, Department of Film, Imperial War Museum, London; Valentin Senger, Frankfurt; Dr. Hugo Stehkemper, Stadtarchiv, Cologne; Rolf Steinberg, Berlin (West); Wolfgang Streubel, Ullstein Bilderdienst, Berlin (West); Glen Sweeting, Aeronautics Department, National Air and Space Museum, Washington, D.C.; Dr. Friedrich Terveen, Landesbildstelle, Berlin (West); Renée and Ulrich von Thüna, Bonn; Marek Webb, Head Archivist, Yivo Institute, New York; Paul White, Audio-Visual Division, National Archives, Washington, D.C.; Dr. Bernd Wiersch, Volkswagenwerk, Wolfsburg, Federal Republic of Germany; M. Willis, Department of Photographs, Imperial War Museum, London.

The index for this book was prepared by Nicholas J. Anthony.